M000216201

★★ THE MIGHTY ★★
GENERALS

A STORY OF

BASKETBALL CHAMPIONSHIPS AND

RACIAL UNITY IN THE DEEP SOUTH

Mike Chibbaro

THIRTY-SEVEN
PUBLISHING

P.O. Box 3714
Greenville, SC 29608

www.thirtysevenpublishing.com

Copyright 2019 © by Mike Chibbaro
Second Printing January 2020

All RIGHTS RESERVED
No part of this publication may be reproduced, stored in a retrieval
system or transmitted, in any form or by any means—electronic,
mechanical, photocopying, recording, or otherwise—without prior
written permission.

For information about special discounts for bulk purchases,
please contact Thirty-Seven Publishing.

Cover design: J.J. Puryear

Copyediting: Amanda Capps

Page Layout: Michael Seymour

Cover photo displays actual basketball used in
1970 SC 4A State Championship Game

ISBN - 978-1-7923-2142-9
Library of Congress Cataloging-in-Publication Data

Dedication

This book is dedicated to all the students, teachers, administrators, parents and community leaders who courageously committed to creating a unified school system in Greenville County in 1970. Without your resolve, the story of *The Mighty Generals* would not have been possible.

Author's Note

In attempting to document the story of *The Mighty Generals*, I relied heavily on the "best recollections" of former coaches, players, students, teachers and others who attempted to recall their memories from 50 years back. I also conducted an exhaustive review of newspaper articles, high school yearbooks and anything else I could find that helped me piece together the story. In certain instances and for the sole purpose of making the story more readable, I have reconstructed conversations as they most likely occurred. These conversations are in alignment with my overall research, but I certainly cannot attest to the absolute accuracy of every word that may be placed within the quotation marks. Therefore, I ask for your understanding and indulgence. My purpose is for you, the reader, to share in the experiences of those who contributed to these historic events.

Certain passages in this book that have been reprinted may have been edited for brevity and clarity. This includes, but is not limited to newspaper articles, book excerpts, transcripts and letters. In all cases, these minor revisions were performed with great care to preserve the meaning intended by the original writers.

Contents

Preface

Sport has the power to change the world. It has the power to inspire. It has the power to unite people in a way that little else does. It speaks to youth in a language they understand. Sport can create hope where once there was only despair. It is more powerful than government in breaking down racial barriers.

Nelson Mandela

Columbia, South Carolina
March 7, 1971

It was close to 1 a.m., and the Wade Hampton Generals boys basketball team had bedded down for the evening at the Golden Eagle Motor Inn on the corner of Main and Elmwood Streets in downtown Columbia, South Carolina. A couple of hours earlier and a few blocks away, the team had captured its second consecutive state 4A high school basketball championship. Shortly before midnight, the Generals defeated a powerful Dreher High School team that featured future Basketball Hall of Famer Alexander English.

The boys were crammed four to a room, two per double bed. They were given clear instructions by Head Coach Johnny Ross not to leave their rooms and to meet first thing in the morning for a pancake breakfast at the Motor Inn's restaurant. After breakfast, they would board the school's activity bus for their triumphant 100-mile Sunday morning ride back to their hometown of Greenville.

Sleep, however, was not on the boys' agenda, and who could blame them? They were euphoric, riding a wave of teenage adrenaline fueled by the act of cutting down the nets after their second consecutive state basketball championship.

Less than two years earlier, some of the players on the Wade Hampton team didn't know one another. They grew up in different sections of town, attended different schools and played for different teams. With the impetus provided by the federal government, they would become the first team in the school's history to include both white and black players.

On May 17, 1954, the United States Supreme Court ruled in the landmark *Brown v. Board of Education* case that dual school systems for white and blacks were unconstitutional. Sixteen years after *Brown v. Board of Education*, federal government officials had reached the end of their patience with the lack of progress shown by the Greenville County School District's implementation of school desegregation. County school administrators were emphatically told that they would integrate their public schools, and they would do it immediately; otherwise, they would lose all federal funding. On February 17, 1970, approximately 12,000 of Greenville County's 57,000 students were reassigned to ensure an 80-20 white to black mix in all schools, a ratio intended to mirror that of the general population of Greenville County.

At the time of the mandated integration, the 1969-70 Wade Hampton boys basketball team was two-thirds of the way through its season and had posted a modest record of 11 wins and seven losses. They were facing an uphill battle to earn a spot in the Class 4A playoffs.

School integration closed the county's five black high schools, which led to the addition of several talented black athletes to Wade Hampton's roster, including 6'7" 225-pound Clyde Mayes, who had been a dominant player at the all-black Beck High School. Once Mayes joined the Generals, Wade Hampton would go on to win 33 of its next 35 games and capture back-to-back state championships while becoming one of the most dominant high school basketball teams ever produced in South Carolina.

The Generals basketball team was comprised of good kids, not prone to destructive mischief. Coach Ross had frequently and publicly praised them for their character, leadership and discipline—but on this evening—in a rare act of disobedience, a handful of them would ignore their coach's orders. The four walls of the rooms at the Golden Eagle Motor Inn could not contain the exuberance of these teenage boys.

Team Co-Captain Norman MacDonald recalled over four decades later: "We just were so excited and happy, we didn't want to go to bed, so we snuck out of our rooms and just started walking through the streets of Columbia. We weren't going anywhere or looking for any trouble, and we didn't have any money. We were just happy to have won our second state championship and didn't want the night to end."

Their journey had begun like many successful teams, with an odd convergence of lives: coaches and young boys from different walks of life brought together in the uncertain and turbulent post-integration Civil Rights Era. United in a singular purpose, they put aside cultural and racial differences, and in the early morning hours of March 1971, on the deserted streets of the state capital, they celebrated with a late-night victory walk.

They walked as teammates. They walked as friends. This is their story.

1
History

A nation that forgets its past can function no better than an individual with amnesia.

Historian David McCullough

In the winter of 1969, the game of basketball across America appeared on the surface to be a fully integrated sport. Willis Reed emerged from a rural farm in northern Louisiana to captain the '69-70 NBA Champion New York Knicks. A graduate of Grambling State University, Reed earned the NBA's 1970 Most Valuable Player Award, marking the 10th consecutive year the trophy was won by a black athlete. The starting five for the '69-70 Knicks included three black players, Reed, Walt "Clyde" Frazier and Dick Barnett. They were joined by future U.S. Senator and Rhodes Scholar Bill Bradley and former Major League Baseball pitcher Dave DeBusschere to form the nucleus of a team known for its unity and cohesiveness.

In the college ranks, UCLA won its sixth of 10 titles under the leadership of legendary Coach John Wooden. Three of the starters on the '69-70 championship team were black: Curtis Rowe, Sidney Wicks and Henry Bibby. All five starters on the team finished the year with double-figure scoring averages evidencing the unselfish and unified nature of this integrated championship team.

In Greenville, South Carolina, however, basketball was a game that whites and blacks, for the most part, played on separate courts. On any given Saturday morning at the Cleveland Street YMCA, doz-

1

ens of youths from across Greenville filled the Y's three tile-floor courts as they participated in a citywide church league basketball program. Absent an occasional black youth from one of the local Catholic congregations, the racial composition of these games mirrored the all-white congregations at churches like Buncombe Street Methodist, First Baptist Church, Sans Souci Baptist and Christ Episcopal Church. In the city's mill communities, recreational basketball leagues were restricted to whites only.

Blacks played pickup basketball on a series of outdoor neighborhood courts or in local inner-city community centers or gyms at the black schools. Only on rare occasions was a white basketball player confident enough in his game to infiltrate one of these highly competitive environments.

By 1969, a small number of black students had enrolled in Greenville's white high schools under the school district's "freedom of choice plan," a program that allowed black families to make summertime petitions to get their children into white schools. Denials of these requests were as frequent as approvals. The limited impact of the plan in Greenville County was evidenced by the makeup of local high school basketball teams in 1969.

As the Christmas break neared, eight area teams (Wade Hampton, Greenville, J.L. Mann, Carolina, Easley, Parker, Palmetto and Hillcrest) prepared to play in the annual three-day Greenville Christmas Invitational Tournament at the 6,500-seat Memorial Auditorium. Of the approximately 100 players participating in the event, fewer than 10 were black. Wade Hampton's team consisted of 12 white players.

The county's five black high schools had no such similar holiday invitational tournament and were in the midst of playing out their schedule against the other all-black high schools across the area.

Press coverage for the predominately white schools was extensive. The Friday morning edition of *The Greenville News* on December 19, 1969, featured a lengthy four-column story on page 1 of the sports section detailing the results of first round games of the Christmas Invitational as well as highlighting the upcoming semifinal match-ups. The article included detailed quotes from winning and losing coaches, along with two large action photos from the games.

By comparison, the bottom of page 4 of the sports section contained two brief sentences describing Beck High School's 102-50 win over Brewer High School. Beck's star center Clyde Mayes scored a remarkable 32 points and grabbed 29 rebounds in a game in which he most certainly saw limited second-half playing time. Throughout the season, coverage of the local black high schools remained inconsistent and sparse, limited typically to a box score and a few meager sentences. This information was always placed in an inconspicuous location on a later page within the sports section.

Six years earlier, Dr. Martin Luther King Jr. delivered his famous "I Have a Dream" speech on the steps of the Lincoln Memorial in Washington, D.C. Five years earlier, President Lyndon Johnson signed into law the Civil Rights Act of 1964, which officially outlawed discrimination based on race. Still, in Greenville, South Carolina, like many Southern towns in 1969, blacks and whites continued to live in segregated neighborhoods, attend separate schools, worship at their own churches and play the game of basketball with people of their own skin color.

Around this time, Jacqueline Woodson was splitting her childhood years between Brooklyn, New York, and Greenville. Woodson published a *New York Times* best-selling collection of poems that reflected memories of her childhood. She attended Sterling High

School and lived in Greenville's Nicholtown community, the same neighborhood that was home to Wade Hampton's future basketball star, Clyde Mayes. The following poem recounts a childhood memory of going to a fabric store in Downtown Greenville where she and her grandmother found a rare exception to the otherwise segregated society of Greenville.

"the fabric store"

Some Fridays, we walk to downtown Greenville where
there are some clothing stores, some restaurants,
a motel and the five-and-dime store but
my grandmother won't take us
into any of those places anymore.
Even the five-and-dime, which isn't segregated now
but where a woman is paid, my grandmother says,
to follow colored people around in case they try to
steal something. We don't go into the restaurants
because they always seat us near the kitchen.
When we go downtown,
we go to the fabric store, where the white woman
knows my grandmother from back in Anderson, asks
How's Gunnar doing and your girls in New York?
She rolls fabric out for my grandmother
to rub between her fingers.
They discuss drape and nap and where to cinch
the waist on a skirt for a child.
At the fabric store, we are not Colored
or Negro. We are not thieves or shameful
or something to be hidden away.
At the fabric store, we're just people.

————————

The town of Greenville, South Carolina, came into existence around 1770, when Richard Pearis, a native of Ireland whose family settled in the Shenandoah Valley area of Virginia, obtained a 12-square-mile tract of land in the area that is now Greenville County from the native Cherokee Indians. Historians have debated on the tactics Pearis used to obtain this land. Some believe he provided liquor to the Indians, leaving them intoxicated to the point of willingly signing over large blocks of land to him. Others believe Pearis was given the land as a gift by the Cherokees.

Pearis established his new plantation home in the area of modern-day South Main Street, near the current Greenville City Hall. He built a gristmill, a sawmill and a trading post along the banks of the Reedy River. Pearis brought with him a dozen African-American slaves to help establish his home and businesses. Other white settlers were quickly attracted to Greenville, and typically, they brought along their slaves. In addition to being a trading post along the Reedy River, Greenville became a popular summer resort vacation spot. Wealthy Low Country residents traveled to Greenville to escape the oppressive summer heat.

During the American Revolution, Pearis joined Native Americans in fighting for the British. After the war, the victorious Patriots destroyed Pearis's home and businesses and imprisoned him in Charleston for several months. After his release, Pearis spent the remainder of his life in the Bahamas where he died in 1794. He never returned to the Upstate, but a reminder of his legacy remains in Greenville—the stand-alone mountain about five miles from downtown that bears his name: Paris Mountain (spelled without the "e").

After the Revolutionary War, the new state of South Carolina took the land previously claimed by the Cherokees and other early settlers and began to distribute it to Patriot soldiers as payment for their wartime services. Greenville most likely drew its name from Revolutionary War hero Major General Nathanael Greene.

In the early 1800s, Vardry McBee, a 40-year-old tanner and merchant from Lincolnton, North Carolina, acquired over 11,000 acres in the Greenville area. McBee cast a bold vision for the future of the Greenville community. He provided land for the building of the city's first schools and churches and opened a rock quarry, along with several mills, a tannery and a large general store. A bronze statue on Main Street in Downtown Greenville today commemorates McBee as "the father of Greenville."

By 1860, the population of Greenville had grown to 21,892, which included 7,049 slaves and 212 freed slaves. Union General William T. Sherman destroyed much of South Carolina's capital city of Columbia as part of his Carolinas Campaign, but Greenville was spared from much of the physical devastation of the Civil War. Nevertheless, Confederate troops returned to Greenville to find the city in poor shape from disregard and disease. All of Greenville's slaves had been set free, and Greenville, like the rest of the South, was under Union guard. The Union troops were to oversee the orderly rebuilding of the South. It was during this time that blacks began to seek training and education.

Charles T. Hopkins, who had been a slave for over 50 years, founded the first school for blacks in Greenville in 1866. Hopkins learned to read and write through "chance opportunity." He was described as an amiable, virtuous and godly man who was trusted by the white community. Hopkins raised $260 to fund the opening of the first school for blacks, which was located in a single room in an abandoned hotel on Main Street. It was there that Hopkins and two assistants began teaching spelling and reading to 60-70 black children. From these humble beginnings, the formal education of blacks in Greenville County began.

"Reconstruction" refers to the post-Civil War period in American history from 1865 to 1877. Under Reconstruction, Southern states were divided into five military districts with each being assigned a Republican governor. Author and historian Henry Louis Gates Jr. summarized this era in *Stony the Road: Reconstruction, White Supremacy, and the Rise of Jim Crow*, when he wrote, "…the period after the Civil War when the United States, at least in theory, attempted to come to terms with its original sin of slavery." Blacks began to gain political influence and representation under Reconstruction. In the first post-Civil War state legislature in South Carolina, blacks actually held a majority position with 88 delegates as compared to 77 white representatives.

The efforts of black citizens to become educated grew during Reconstruction but were met with hostility by many whites who saw the education of blacks as a threat to the workforce needed for the South's primary means of commerce: farming. During Reconstruction, however, black-owned businesses began to emerge with frequency.

Leola Clement Robinson-Simpson wrote in *Black America Series—Greenville, South Carolina*, about the influence of black businesses in the Greenville Community in the 1800s:

> *Though Greenville was a traditional mill town, employment in manufacturing tended to be restricted to*

the white populace. However, in the 1870s, there were 70 African American businesses on Main Street in Greenville, including six barbershops, three retail stores, one meat market, and three restaurants, and the only brick manufacturing company in town was owned by an African American businessman. African American business-es flourished and spread to adjacent downtown streets. Thrifty and business-savvy African Americans accumu-lated sizable amounts of property and wealth though re-cently freed from bondage.

A number of factors contributed to the end of Reconstruction in-cluding the withdrawal of Union troops from the South, an econom-ic depression in 1874 and the emergence of violent white suprema-cist groups like the Ku Klux Klan. A movement in Southern states emerged to reclaim the "glory of the South," which led to the enact-ment of laws and codes designed to segregate whites and blacks. The impact of the end of Reconstruction was felt on Greenville's black business owners as described by Leola Clement Robinson-Simpson:

Unfortunately, with the rise of Jim Crow and the Klan in the 1900s, African Americans lost control over the tra-ditional barbering, hacking, and drayage industries, as well as over the downtown stores in Greenville. As the older established African Americans passed away from the scene, they were systematically replaced by whites. It was during this sad era in Greenville's history that whites began the process of wrestling from the hands of African Americans the prized businesses and property that had been owned by African American families since the early 1800s.

"Jim Crow" was a term commonly associated with any law in the Southern states that promoted segregation between whites and blacks. Jim Crow laws began to emerge shortly after the end of Reconstruction (1877) and began to slowly disappear only with the onset of the American Civil Rights Movement in the 1950s. The name "Jim Crow" came from a traveling minstrel act first performed by Thomas Dartmouth "Daddy" Rice and subsequently copied by a number of other road shows. The programs included comedy skits, music, dancing and variety acts performed by "black-faced" Caucasian actors. The shows were designed to depict a typical African-American as lazy, intellectually challenged and generally less of a human than a white counterpart. One of the more popular traveling Jim Crow minstrel shows, the "Al Field Minstrels," made an annual appearance to sold-out crowds in Greenville at either the Grand Opera House or Textile Hall during the early 1900s.

Jim Crow laws were founded upon an underlying belief in white supremacy. They were spawned during an era when whites feared losing jobs to blacks, crimes were frequently attributed to innocent blacks and the media fed a bias against blacks through their depiction of various alleged behaviors and crimes.

In 1890, the Louisiana General Assembly passed a law that prohibited blacks and whites from traveling together in the same railroad cars. The ruling was challenged in the landmark case *Plessy v. Ferguson*, but the U.S. Supreme Court upheld the law and stated that public facilities for whites and blacks could be "separate but equal." Shortly thereafter, the state of Mississippi began to restrict voting rights of blacks, a practice adopted throughout the South that led to a significant drop in the number of eligible black voters.

Jim Crow laws placed restrictions on nearly every aspect of life in the South. In South Carolina's textile mills, blacks and whites were not permitted to work in the same room together. Signs bearing the label "white" or "black" hung over separate water fountains, pay phones and ticket booths. Curfews in many cities forced blacks inside their homes after 10 p.m. In courtrooms in Atlanta, white witnesses and black witnesses took their oaths on separate Bibles. Prisons, hospitals, parks, orphanages and schools were segregated facilities.

Isabel Wilkerson, in her Pulitzer Prize-winning book, *The Warmth of Other Suns*, explains the generational impact of Jim Crow laws in the South:

> *Younger blacks could see the contradictions in their world—that, sixty, seventy, eighty years after Abraham Lincoln signed the Emancipation Proclamation, they still had to step off the sidewalk when a white person approached, were banished to jobs nobody else wanted no matter their skill or ambition, couldn't vote, but could be hanged on suspicion of the pettiest infraction.*
>
> *These were the facts of their lives:*
>
> *There were days when whites could go to the amusement park and a day when blacks could go, if they were permitted at all. There were white elevators and colored elevators (meaning the freight elevators in back); white train platforms and colored train platforms. There were white ambulances and colored ambulances to ferry the sick...There were white waiting rooms and colored wait-*

ing rooms in any conceivable place where a person might have to wait for something, from the bus depot to the doctor's office...

Throughout the South, the conventional rules of the road did not apply when a colored motorist was behind the wheel. If he reached an intersection first, he had to let the white motorist go ahead of him. He could not pass a white motorist on the road no matter how slowly the white motorist was going and had to take extreme caution to avoid an accident because he would likely be blamed no matter who was at fault. In everyday interactions a black person could not contradict a white person or speak unless spoken to first. A black person could not be the first to offer to shake a white person's hand. A handshake could occur only if a white person so gestured, leaving many people having never shaken hands with a person of the other race...

Jim Crow would not get a proper burial until the enactment of federal legislation, the Civil Rights Act of 1964, which was nonetheless resisted years after its passage as vigorously as Reconstruction had been and would not fully take hold in many parts of the South until well into the 1970s.

Two memorable events stand out as being catalytic to the advancement of civil rights in Greenville. The first occurred two months before Jackie Robinson of the Brooklyn Dodgers became the first African-American to play baseball in the major leagues. The second related to a post-retirement visit by the legendary Robinson to Greenville.

In 1947, Greenville drew national attention for a highly publicized lynching of a black man accused of a crime. At about 9 p.m. on the evening of February 16, 1947, Yellow Cab driver Thomas Brown picked up a fare at the corner of Markley and Calhoun Streets in Greenville's West End of town and drove him approximately 18 miles to his home in Liberty, South Carolina. According to the FBI and local police investigation files, about an hour after picking up the fare in Downtown Greenville, Brown was found badly beaten and bleeding alongside Old Liberty-Pickens Road.

Police reports indicated that footprints from the site where Brown's body was found led to the home of 24-year-old Willie Earle, approximately a mile away. Police stated they found money taken from Brown and a bloodstained jacket and knife at Earle's home.

Earle dropped out of school when he was 10 and suffered from epilepsy, a condition that often made it difficult for him to find steady work. Brown, the cab driver, was a 48-year-old disabled veteran from World War I. Two weeks before his death, Brown's mother passed away. He was described as a slight man who did not drink or smoke and who was a positive influence on his fellow taxi drivers.

Earle was arrested and placed in a small cell at the county jail in Pickens late on Sunday evening. As word spread about Earle's alleged murder of a cabbie, local drivers from several cab companies began to gather at the Yellow Cab offices on West Court Street in Downtown Greenville. One driver reportedly purchased a quart of whiskey, which was passed around among the cab drivers as they began to talk about the reported beating.

Before long, a group of 31 white men, including 28 cab drivers, a café operator and two local businessmen, loaded up in their vehicles and caravanned to the Pickens County jail. At approximately 5 a.m., the angry posse of armed men banged on the door of the jail and demanded that Earle be handed over to them.

In 2003, staff writer Dan Hoover of *The Greenville News* thoroughly researched and reported on the death of Willie Earle. The following is his account of what transpired after the men arrived at the jail.

> *Whether the unusual sound of so many vehicles at 5 a.m. awakened jailer J.E. Gilstrap, 62, at the red-brick turreted jailhouse is not known, but he responded to the pounding on the ground floor apartment's door.*
>
> *He would tell the sheriff that many wore caps like those of cab drivers and the street was filled with taxis, according to police records.*
>
> *They wanted the man who cut Brown. Gilstrap, in his nightclothes, unarmed and faced with at least two shotguns, gave him up.*
>
> *An hour later, an anonymous call to a black funeral home in Greenville announces the whereabouts of a "Negro's" body on Bramlett Road, an isolated unpaved road west of town. The mortician relayed the information to Coroner J.O. Turner, who found the body.*
>
> *It was still warm…Earle had been beaten, slashed and shot, at least twice, by shotgun blasts.*

Unlike the majority of other murders of blacks in the Jim Crow South, the beating of Willie Earle would not be swept aside and viewed as an appropriate and just action taken by a group of whites. Governor Strom Thurmond promptly issued the following statement, which was a bit unusual for the governor of a Southern state during this era: "I do not favor lynching, and I shall exert every resource at my command to apprehend all persons who may be involved in such a flagrant violation of the law." (Note: the term "lynching" not only included deaths by hanging, but also any death caused by a mob that operated outside any legal authority.)

Local law enforcement officials, with assistance from the FBI and state agencies, quickly arrested all 31 of Earle's alleged assailants. Twenty-six of the 31 signed confessions shortly after their arrests. Their confessions were detailed regarding their plans to abduct Earle. Several of the confessors explained that after beating and stabbing Earle, one member of the group, R. Carlos Hurd, a 45-year-old taxi dispatcher, had placed a shotgun against Earle's head and fired twice.

All 31 of the defendants were released on individual $2,500 bonds. While the investigation proceeded, the beaten cab driver, Thomas Brown, died at St. Francis Hospital in Greenville from the wounds he had received the previous night.

The trial of the mob members began on May 12 and put Greenville under the microscope of the national media. *Life Magazine* dispatched a reporter, a photographer and a sketch artist to Greenville and would ultimately publish a lengthy feature on the trial in their June 6, 1947 issue. *The New Yorker* also sent a senior reporter to cover the trial.

The jury consisted of 12 white males, including seven textile workers, two salesmen, a farmer, a truck driver and a mechanic. They were sequestered for the nine days of the trial and spent their nights at the nearby Poinsett Hotel, a stone's throw from where the accused devised their late-night plan to extract Earle from the Liberty jail. One of the many unanswered questions from the trial was why it was not moved to a neighboring town to help relieve potential bias of the jurors and also to protect the jurors in the event they rendered an unpopular verdict.

Thirty-seven-year-old Judge J. Robert Martin Jr. of the 13th Judicial Circuit Court presided. Martin, from the outset, let it be known that he would not allow the trial to be centered on race. He warned the attorneys about injecting any racially oriented comments, an admonition that was repeatedly ignored by defense attorneys. The most egregious of these statements was made by defense attorney John Bolt Culbertson when he proclaimed, "Willie Earle is dead, and I wish more like him were dead." Martin quickly told Culbertson that he was out of order and then directed the jury to do the impossible and forget those remarks had been made.

The trial was held at the Greenville County Courthouse on Main Street next to the Poinsett Hotel. The main floor of the courtroom consisted of approximately 300 chairs, all reserved for white attendees. The front rows were allocated for the 31 defendants. Nearly all of the family members of the defendants were present for the trial each day. Only a handful of black residents were able to make it into the courtroom, and they were seated together in the balcony, along with two black reporters representing Northern black newspapers. Each day of the nine-day trial, the courtroom was overflowing with spectators.

The State's case relied heavily on the statements given by 26 of the defendants. It produced no eyewitness testimony to the crime committed against Earle and provided very limited corroborating evidence to the confessions. Subsequent analysis of the prosecution's handling of the case revealed a handful of legal miscues that weakened the legal foundation of their prosecution.

Defense attorneys based their arguments around the inappropriate interference in the case by the FBI, often referred to as "Northern interlopers." They claimed that the investigation should have been a "Southern matter" and that the involvement from the FBI and other outside parties tainted jurisprudence. They also attempted to discredit the confessions claiming all of the confessors were coerced into giving their statements.

After closing arguments by the attorneys, Judge Martin delivered a lengthy 5,000-word charge to the jury before it began deliberations. He reminded the jury that the "State cannot establish a conspiracy by the alleged statements of the individual defendants alone." In other words, the statement of one defendant could not be used against another. The jury weighed the evidence in chambers for just a little over five hours. After reading the verdict, Judge Martin handed it to the bailiff to be read. Hoover's 2003 article in *The Greenville News* describes the scene when the verdict was returned.

> *With a spring rain pelting down outside, jurors began deliberation. At 8:33 p.m., after five hours and 15 minutes, including dinner, they buzzed bailiffs to signify a verdict had been reached. (Judge) Martin delayed its reading until he returned from dinner.*
>
> *With more than 500 people in the courtroom, verdicts were read beginning at 10:23 p.m.*
>
> *Not guilty on all counts.*

Rebecca West, a British journalist who had reported on the Nuremberg Trials the year before, covered the trial for *The New Yorker*. In her lengthy piece, "Opera in Greenville," she described the scene in the courtroom after the readings of the verdicts.

As soon as the clerk had read the verdicts aloud and the Judge had left the bench and the courtroom, which he did without thanking the jury, the courtroom became, in a flash something else. It might have been a honky-tonk, a tourist camp... The Greenville citizens who had come as spectators were filing out quietly and thoughtfully. Whatever their opinions were, they were not to recover their usual spirits for some days. As they went, they looked over their shoulders at the knot of orgiastic joy that had instantly been formed by the defendants and their supporters.

The defendants in the lynching trial of Willie Earle celebrate with their families after the jury issues a not-guilty verdict in the Greenville County Courthouse on the evening of May 21, 1947.
(Photo courtesy of AP Images)

While the assailants of Willie Earle were never convicted, many saw the trial in Greenville as a landmark case marking one of the first recorded attempts to bring justice to the accused white assailants of a black man. A *Life Magazine* article on the trial summarized its ending as follows:

> *The trial did not end in a way to satisfy those who believe that democracy means what it says, regardless of the color of a man's skin. The jury—after hearing the 26 signed statements, after hearing no word of defense testimony and almost no defense argument except some old-fashioned pleas for white supremacy—voted in a mere five and a quarter hours to acquit the defendants. Then, as soon as the trial was declared ended and the judge had departed from the courtroom, pandemonium broke loose when friends, relatives and just plain spectators congratulated the defendants.*
>
> *But history had been made nonetheless. At the urging of Governor Thurmond, white officers of the law had done their best to investigate the lynch murder of a Negro. Special Prosecutor Sam R. Wyatt had presented the case in court with all of his skill. Judge J. Robert Martin Jr. had conducted the trial from start to finish with admirable fairness. It was clear that the South could no longer be considered 100% safe for a lynch mob, or at least that lynching could not be kept 100% secret.*

Two weeks after the lynching of Willie Earle, Hawley Lynn, a white Methodist pastor in Earle's hometown of Liberty, preached a courageous sermon to his congregation at Grace Methodist Church. In *Who Lynched Willie Earle? Preaching to Confront Racism*, author Will Willimon details the story behind Lynn's sermon and includes the text of the sermon in the book. The following is a brief excerpt from the message Reverend Lynn delivered at Grace Methodist Church on March 2, 1947:

> *The lynching of Willie Earle didn't begin on February 17; it began a long time ago; it began when his father and mother taught him that he was black folks and must always tip his hat and get out the way of white folks. It began when he walked to school, because there were not uses for his kind, and hurried home to hoe cotton or pick it on a tenant farm. It began when he learned that there were only certain kinds of jobs that black men could fill, and certain foods they could afford, chiefly the 3Ms, fat meat, meal, and molasses...*

Lynn's sermon openly criticized Jim Crow laws and contained a detailed historical discussion of the roots of democracy in the United States, noting that the tyranny of white supremacy could not be allowed to continue in our country. In his analysis of the sermon, Willimon stated the following:

> *The most remarkable aspect of Hawley's sermon, Who Lynched Willie Earle? is that it was preached. Unlike most South Carolina pastors, Hawley was not silent...Hawley spoke up. The lesson we preachers learn from Hawley Lynn? He spoke.*

The Constitution of the State of South Carolina provided a compensatory payment of not less than $2,000 to the surviving family of anyone lynched in the state. Tessie Earle, the mother of Willie Earle, petitioned the Court for this payment, and her request was initially denied by the county attorney, who claimed there was a lack of proof that Earle's death came from lynching. Three years after the death of her son, Tessie Earle finally received the minimum payment of $2,000.

In the most tragic of ways, the lynching of Willie Earle began to sow seeds in the Greenville community for needed racial reforms. Prominent white citizens were concerned about the impact of incidents like this upon their desire to have Greenville seen as a progressive and modern city that would be inviting to economic investments. After the trial, defense attorney John Bolt Culbertson became a staunch advocate for civil rights. He became the first white member of the state's branch of the National Association for the Advancement of Colored People (NAACP) and was lauded by *Ebony* magazine as "the bravest politician in South Carolina." He also assisted Tessie Earle in obtaining her $2,000 civil award.

Four years after the lynching of Willie Earle, the state of South Carolina passed its first statute criminalizing lynching. The bill was introduced by Representative Ernest Hollings in 1951 and stated that mob action resulting in death would be punishable by death.

On October 25, 1959, Jackie Robinson was invited to Greenville to give the keynote address at the conclusion of a regional meeting of the NAACP. After the completion of his historic nine-year major league baseball career, Robinson became a traveling spokesperson for the NAACP. In Greenville, Robinson spoke to an audience of approximately 1,700 at the newly constructed Greenville Memorial Auditorium. Gil Rowland reported on the event for *The Greenville News* and noted, "The writer saw only two white persons in the audience, one of them a radio station reporter."

Robinson encouraged his Greenville audience to work through the NAACP to help bring about freedom for all people. He shared a number of personal examples of discrimination from his own life and said, "I don't want my kids to have to go through this kind of thing, and I don't want your kids to either."

When Robinson was escorted back to the airport later that day for his departure, he took his seat, along with a handful of representatives of the local chapter of the NAACP, in the main lounge. The group was asked by an armed airport official to vacate the "whites only" waiting area. A similar scene had occurred with the delegation sent to pick up Robinson on his arrival at the airport earlier in the day. When Robinson and his companions refused to move, a local police officer was summoned onto the scene.

Robinson and the NAACP representatives with him informed the officer that four years earlier the Interstate Commerce Commission (ICC) had ruled that segregation of interstate travelers in public waiting rooms was unlawful. They also told the officer they did not desire to make a disturbance, but since the airport was a federally funded facility and subject to the rules of the ICC, they wanted to know under what Greenville law they were acting when they asked them to move.

Two weeks after the incident, Robinson shared his memories of the Greenville experience to a reporter for an African-American newspaper in Baltimore: "The officer apparently was perplexed, for after making a quick telephone call, he decided to quit the scene. We stayed on in the main waiting room until our plane arrived. And before we boarded for our flight to New York, we were greatly heartened by a crowd of well-wishers who entered the terminal as a means of expressing their support for our stand."

In addition to Robinson's incident earlier in 1959, a black civilian U.S. Air Force employee, Richard Henry from Michigan, had been forcibly removed from the white waiting room at the downtown airport. Henry retained the legal services of Greenville attorney Willie T. Smith and Columbia attorney Lincoln Jenkins and filed a suit against the airport.

In April 2013, *The State* newspaper published an article explaining the connection between Robinson's airport experience and the advancement of the Civil Rights Movement in Greenville. The article credits the courage of Robinson and the others who were with him that day at the airport for providing the inspiration for black Greenvillians to publicly stand up to the inequities of segregation. By December of 1959, local black leaders had put together plans for a historic protest march on the airport to call for an end to segregation.

One of the Greenvillians with Robinson in October was the Reverend James Hall, an energetic and charismatic 28-year-old pastor from Springfield Baptist Church. Hall was the driving force behind the historic airport march, which he referred to as a "prayer pilgrimage." Hall, who was only 25 when he took over as lead pastor at Springfield in 1956, became the visionary leader for the Civil Rights Movement in Greenville. He would establish an NAACP youth council and go on to become a lifelong mentor to one of its members, the man we know today as the Reverend Jesse Jackson; at the time, Jackson was a senior at Sterling High School.

Under Hall's leadership, approximately 1,000 Greenvillians—including Jesse Jackson, who was home from college—marched from Springfield Baptist Church on McBee Street to the airport on Pleasantburg Drive on January 1, 1960. *The Greenville News* described the tense atmosphere surrounding the march:

> *Probably 70 plainclothes officers, including city detectives, deputies and officers of the South Carolina Law Enforcement Division, and many uniformed city officers, circulated among the crowd alert for the start of any disturbance.*
>
> *At least nine men identified by officers as being or once being connected with Ku Klux Klan organizations were checked personally by officers.*

At approximately 4:30 p.m., 15 of the representatives from the protest were invited into the airport to read a resolution that had been prepared. As the delegates were ushered inside, those remaining outside began to sing "America" while standing in a slight flurry of snow or sleet.

The Reverend Matthew McCollough from Orangeburg read the resolution, which included the following:

> *We will not make a pretense of being satisfied with the crumbs of citizenship while other(s) enjoy the whole loaf only by right of a white-skinned birth...with faith in this nation and its God, we shall not relent, we shall not rest, we shall not compromise, we shall not be satisfied until every vestige of racial discrimination and segregation has been eliminated from all*

aspects of our public life.

The Greenville News stated, "There were no incidents to interrupt the ceremony or at any time during the afternoon."

Protesters march on the Greenville airport on January 1, 1960, in what was referred to as a "prayer pilgrimage" inspired by the discriminatory treatment of Jackie Robinson at the airport in October 1959. Over 1,000 men, women and children marched in protest of segregation.
(Photo courtesy of Upcountry History Museum, James Wilson Collection)

Following the airport march, sit-ins at downtown lunch counters, local libraries and public swimming facilities began to occur on a regular basis in Greenville. Many of these were led by the NAACP youth council, which included the Reverend Jackson. Several arrests and additional sit-ins resulted from the activities of the students. Local attorneys Willie T. Smith and Donald Sampson received legal support from the NAACP's high-powered team of Thurgood Marshall and Jack Greenberg, as they filed suits against the city of Greenville and the local library. The sit-ins, arrests and lawsuits became the driving forces behind desegregating Greenville.

Despite all the local and national efforts that aimed to eradicate the inequities of the "separate but equal" doctrine in the 1960s, the schools of Greenville County remained segregated. With the dawning of a new decade, this was about to change.

2
Defiance or Compliance

We have come to the crossroads where we must choose between defiance and compliance.

South Carolina Governor Robert McNair

January 1970

Edna Mae Mayes sat at her kitchen table in her home at 500 Glenn Road in Greenville's Nicholtown community, heartbroken over the fate of her two youngest children. Since her husband left her and moved to New York nearly 15 years earlier, she was determined to provide as normal a life as possible for her three children. During the day, she worked diligently and honorably as a housekeeper for a white family in a nearby wealthy neighborhood. In the evenings, she worked as a nurse's aide at Greenville General Hospital. Her three children excelled in school and athletics, attended church faithfully and stayed out of trouble. They didn't deserve the unfortunate set of circumstances that beset them in the early days of 1970.

The lines of the Greenville County School District's integration plan ran directly through the home of the Mayes family. The plan resulted in the scheduled closing of all the county's black high schools, including J.H. Beck High in Nicholtown. Edna's son Clyde, a junior at Beck, would be assigned to Wade Hampton High School, while Edna's daughter Ruth, a senior, was sent to J.L. Mann High School to complete the final semester of her 12th-grade year.

The splitting of siblings as part of the district's integration plan was uncommon. Concerned friends and family encouraged Edna to appeal the assignments of her children and seek relief that would allow her two high school-age students to attend the same school.

"My mother got an attorney and even appeared before a judge," Edna's son Clyde recalled. "But the judge denied her request and told her that she would have to comply, and my sister and I would have to go to different schools."

The Mayes children, along with over 12,000 other Greenville students, dutifully accepted their new school assignments in the middle of the 1969-70 school year. Beginning on the morning of February 17, 1970, Clyde and his sister would depart from their home in Nicholtown and head in opposite directions on their way to school.

Meanwhile, across town in the Taylors community, John and Barbara Ross contemplated the impact of the district's desegregation plans on their family. On the bright side, John, as the head basketball coach at Wade Hampton High School, would retain his teaching and coaching position there, and his team would be the beneficiary of the transfer of Clyde Mayes—a 6'7" basketball prodigy.

Still, the Ross family did not escape the impact of desegregation. Their oldest daughter Cathy, a quiet blond-haired sixth-grader at Northwood Middle School, was reassigned to Nicholtown Elementary. Previously an all-black elementary school, Nicholtown Elementary was being converted into an integrated sixth-grade facility.

The physical condition of Nicholtown Elementary and its access to resources, like most of the all-black schools in Greenville, was substandard in comparison with Cathy's current school. A 1999 article in *The Greenville News* described Nicholtown Elementary in the following way:

Buildings for black children were not in good shape, and even new schools such as Nicholtown Elementary built in 1950, were not quite complete. Brickwork was not done, and the heating system was so inadequate, children and teachers wore jackets and gloves in the winter. The books were hand-me-downs from the white schools: tattered, torn and outdated.

One family in the Ross's neighborhood, upon learning of the reassignment of their sixth-grade son to Nicholtown, quickly pulled their child from the public school system and enrolled him in an all-white private school. While many parents complained and protested the new school assignments, the Ross family quietly accepted the midyear reassignment of their oldest daughter. Beginning on the morning of February 17, 1970, Cathy boarded an early morning school bus for the seven-mile ride from her home on Tiffany Drive in Taylors to her new school in the heart of the Nicholtown community.

Such was the uncompromising and abrupt upheaval facing students, parents and faculty in the winter of 1970 in Greenville County. On the surface, it appeared sudden, but it was a long time in the making.

———————

On May 17, 1954, the United States Supreme Court ruled in *Brown v. Board of Education* that dual school systems for white and black students were unconstitutional. The unanimous decision overturned the 1896 ruling of *Plessy v. Ferguson*, which allowed for the establishment of "separate but equal" public facilities throughout the nation. The Brown decision stated that public school segregation violated the equal protection granted to all U.S. citizens under the 14th Amendment.

Like in many school districts in the Deep South, change, as a result of the landmark Supreme Court ruling, was slow in Greenville. By 1961, seven years after the Brown decision and 100 years after the attack on Charleston's Fort Sumter by Confederate forces, South Carolina, Alabama and Mississippi were the only three states that had essentially avoided the desegregation of public schools.

The advancement of the integration of the schools in Greenville was given a boost in 1963 through the heroic actions of Abraham Jonas "A.J." Whittenberg, a black auto repair shop owner. Whittenberg was born on a rural farm in southern Greenville County and moved into the city as a youth in 1932. After working a series of manual labor jobs, he opened an auto repair shop and gas station on Anderson Street. His honest reputation and his skill as a mechanic provided a formula for the success of his shop, which served a mix of white and black customers. In a good year, Whittenberg's business reportedly grossed over $100,000, which if adjusted for inflation, would approximate $1 million in today's dollars.

From an early age, Whittenberg's father impressed upon him the importance of exercising his right to vote, even though during Whittenberg's childhood years, blacks in South Carolina were allowed to vote only in presidential elections. His father's inspiration drove Whittenberg to become active in Greenville's local political scene.

Prior to desegregation, the school district was required to maintain separate but equal facilities for whites and blacks. The schools may have been separate, but clearly, they were not equal. While attending a local political function at an all-white school, Whittenberg could not help but recognize the difference between that school and the all-black school attended by his 11-year-old daughter, Elaine, who had recently been reassigned to a different black school. The change would require her to cross a couple of major intersections on her walk to school. The Anderson Street School, a white school, was much closer to the Whittenbergs' home and would have been a safer walk for Elaine.

In an August 1980 interview with *The Greenville News*, Whittenberg recalled his memories of the disparity in white and black schools:

> *I'll never forget this. I was walking in the hall of the Anderson Street School, and in the corner was a stack of books. No names in them they were so new. I thought when I saw those books, Elaine, my little daughter, never had books like that. The books she had were torn. Pages were missing. They'd been used for years in white schools and passed on to the Negro children.*

Validating Whittenberg's concerns is the testimony of Maxine Moragne, who in the 1960s was one of the few black members of the Greenville County School District's administrative staff. Moragne graduated from the all-black Lincoln High School and subsequently attended Morris Brown College in Atlanta before returning to Lincoln as a choral music teacher. While teaching at Lincoln in 1967, Moragne was selected by the school district to work as an elementary music supervisor and consultant. Like Whittenberg, she noticed the differences in the resources being provided to black schools. In 2002,

Moragne granted an interview with Debbie Spear of the Upcountry History Museum and Furman University in which she recalled the specific day she became aware of the disparity in the books being used in black and white schools prior to desegregation.

> *The most glaring thing that I can't until today understand was one day I went to get some music books. And I went to what was supposed to be the depository for the books and I went to the wrong place...When I say I went to the wrong place, I found that I had gotten my books out of the wrong bookroom. And when I asked why, I discovered that not only were the schools segregated, but books were segregated. The books that were being used by the black students were housed in a whole separate building from the books that were used in the white schools.*
>
> *You see the books that were in one room were five or ten years older. They were worn, they were used, they were torn. Pages were missing...You could miss the whole Civil War out of a history book because it was torn out, because the book was so tattered and worn. Those are the books that were relegated to go to what had been the predominately black schools.*

In August of 1963, Whittenberg and five other black parents petitioned the superintendent of the Greenville schools to allow their children to attend white schools. He quickly denied their requests. Whittenberg and the other families engaged attorneys Willie T. Smith and Matthew Perry to file suit in the U.S. District Court petitioning to overturn the superintendent's ruling. Whittenberg explained his realistic understanding of the consequences of his actions and the internal motivation for the suit in the 1980 interview with Dale Perry of *The Greenville News*.

> *I knew what was going to happen in the community. I knew my family was in for some hard times. Things would be dangerous. But I had to do it…I had been on my knees with God too long not to go ahead and do something he told me was right.*

Whittenberg's fears of retribution were soon realized. He told *The Greenville News* about a letter he received shortly after the suit was filed.

> *As long as I live I will never forget the day I opened the mail and somebody had cut a picture of Elaine out of the newspaper. They took a pencil and drew a rope around her neck and wrote, "This is what is going to happen."*

Whittenberg's once thriving auto repair business, located at 600 Anderson Avenue between the Sterling and Sullivan communities, dropped off significantly. White customers fled his shop in anger over the controversial position he had staked. His black customers stopped trading with him for fear they would be fired by their white employers for associating with Whittenberg. He said in *The Greenville News*, "My business dropped way down to where I couldn't make a living."

The threats were not limited to Whittenberg. Writing in *Negroes in Greenville, 1970*, attorney Willie T. Smith said:

Personal harassment became intense after we filed suit. I had all sorts of telephone calls from people who identified themselves as members of the Ku Klux Klan. ...Of course, in the Civil Rights Movement a person gets to the place where these things don't bother him. Usually the harassment is limited to threats. The callers won't identify themselves.

In March of 1964, Whittenberg's case came before federal Judge Robert Martin Jr., a native of Greenville, who had presided over the trial of the 31 white men accused of lynching Willie Earle 17 years earlier. Whittenberg recalled visiting the S.C. Franks Funeral Home in 1947 and viewing the open casket displaying the badly disfigured body of the slain Earle. Whittenberg's historic fight for equality in local schools would be linked to the tragic slaying of Earle through the role of Judge Martin.

Martin overturned the superintendent's ruling and ordered the school district to reconsider the transfer requests and formulate a policy for future applications. Shortly thereafter, Martin issued a consent order, which led to the students being admitted to the white schools. Judge Martin accepted the school board's new policy for "enrollment, assignment and transfer of pupils without regard to race, creed or color." This policy became known as the "freedom of choice" plan and was utilized in Greenville and other parts of the state from 1964 until 1970.

In 2010, Whittenberg's legacy was honored as a new elementary school in Downtown Greenville was dedicated. The A.J. Whittenberg Elementary School of Engineering, a modern 88,000-square-foot facility located a few blocks from where Whittenberg operated his auto garage, is considered to be the most technologically advanced school in the Greenville School District. Annually, the district maintains a long waiting list of students desiring to get into this prestigious school.

The freedom of choice plan allowed for the continuance of a dual education system. The program placed the burden of integration on black parents who were required to apply to the all-white school board if they wanted their children to attend white schools. Their requests were reviewed and either approved or denied, often with little or no explanation to the petitioning parents. By 1969, the freedom of choice plan had resulted in only half of the 100 public schools in Greenville County being racially mixed.

Twelve predominately white high schools existed in the district in 1970. Enrollment in these schools consisted of 13,057 whites and only 838 blacks. Wade Hampton High, the largest high school in the district, had an enrollment of 2,161; only 43 students were black. It is highly unlikely that this was the kind of desegregation the nine Supreme Court justices who ruled on *Brown v. Board of Education* had in mind in 1954.

As a result of Greenville's lack of meaningful progress on school integration, by 1967, the United States Department of Health and Welfare, in line with Title IV of the Civil Rights Act of 1964, threatened to cut all federal funding of Greenville County Schools. Although local opposition to forced segregation remained strong in Greenville, it could not derail the inevitable. In May of 1968, the U.S. Supreme Court, in *Green v. County School Board of New Kent County*, ruled that freedom of choice was an ineffective way to integrate the schools and required local school boards to immediately end dual school systems.

The Greenville school board submitted a revised plan for desegregation to Judge Martin. The board proposed phasing out the freedom of choice plan at the end of the 1970 school year and creating a unitary system starting the following year. Board members hoped to take their time to respond to the Supreme Court ruling, however a separate Supreme Court case (*Alexander v. Holmes County Board of Education*) provided urgent and immediate guidance to school districts, stating: "The obligation of every school district is to terminate dual systems at once and to operate now and hereafter as unitary systems." This ruling was for a case involving 33 different school districts like Greenville that were attempting to postpone the immediate implementation of the Green decision.

On January 19, 1970, Judge Clement Haynsworth, Chief Judge of the United States Court of Appeals for the Fourth Circuit in Richmond, Virginia, ordered the immediate dismantling of Greenville County School District's dual system. The ruling imposed a strict February 9, 1970 deadline (later extended to February 16), forcing massive integration changes to take place in the middle of the school year and effectively ending segregation in Greenville County Schools. Like Judge Martin, Judge Haynsworth was a native of Greenville. In an effort to help prepare his hometown for the significant impact of his ruling, Haynsworth secretly provided an advance copy of the ruling to *The Greenville News* two days prior its official release.

In the wake of the court rulings, Governor Robert McNair, a moderate, told South Carolinians that they had "run out of court and out of time." He stated, "We have come to the crossroads where we must choose between defiance and compliance." McNair strongly encouraged the citizens of South Carolina to comply. When he died in 2007, his son acknowledged in his eulogy that his father's "stand for law and order and public education caused him to be disowned by the rabble-rousing governors of other Southern states."

Greenville School District Superintendent Dr. M.T. Anderson expressed his disappointment in the mandate. The day following the final court ruling, Anderson was quoted in the *Greenville Piedmont*.

> *This drastic action by the court in the middle of the year leaves inadequate time for preparation and raises numerous difficult problems which will result in serious disruption of the education process for thousands of pupils and have adverse effects upon their learning experiences for the rest of the year…However, the court has rendered its decision, and we will of course, make every effort to comply with it.*

Citizens opposed to school integration in Greenville quickly organized and began to mount a desperate all-out effort to retain a segregated school system. Less than a week after the ruling, a group called "Citizens for Freedom of Choice" held a well-publicized meeting at Parker High School in the heart of Greenville's textile mill community. Over 3,000 Greenvillians filled the auditorium, cafeteria and band room at Parker to protest the ruling and discuss options and strategies to avoid compliance. An additional 2,000 upset citizens were turned away due to lack of space at the school. One week later, the group held another rally in Memorial Auditorium drawing more than 3,000 concerned citizens. They opened an office in Downtown Greenville and took out a full-page ad in *The Greenville News* asking for contributions to help with the cost of their fight. The committee requested citizens to drive around town with their headlights turned on as a symbol of their protest of the school's integration plan.

Another anti-integration group, "The Citizens to Prevent Busing Committee," organized a 1,000-car motorcade from Greenville to Columbia. Nearly 3,000 local citizens drove to Columbia on a Sunday afternoon and joined forces with a like-minded group from Darlington, South Carolina. They stood united on the steps of the State House and expressed their displeasure over the forced integration plan. Leaders of the groups handed over signed petitions with over 100,000 names of people who wanted to stop the planned integration of schools in Greenville and Darlington. Twelve of the group's representatives obtained a brief meeting with Governor McNair during which they reportedly demanded immediate corrective action from him. The spokesperson and leader of the group from Greenville was future South Carolina Congressman and Governor Carroll A. Campbell.

Ten of the 11 private schools in Greenville reported that they were flooded with calls from parents interested in transferring their children to their schools immediately. The only private school personnel who indicated their school was not receiving calls about possible transfers were those of St. Anthony's Catholic School, which served the black community's elementary-age children.

Greenville Mayor Cooper White, in his first public comments after the federal desegregation ruling, proclaimed that all four of his children would remain in public schools and attend the schools to which they had been assigned. White, considered a moderate Republican who supported the integration of the schools said, "The court decision has been made, and from what attorneys tell me, there is no room for further debate. It behooves all of us to cooperate in every way possible in the implementation of the court order." Also, on the

Friday before the Monday integration, White invited every minister in the county to a luncheon and asked them to preach a sermon on Sunday encouraging their congregations in their duty to obey the law.

Many black parents also were not pleased with the integration plan. Local pastor H.L. Sullivan, on behalf of a group called "Concerned Black Parents," sent a written petition to the school board with the following requests: 1) that seniors be allowed to finish the school year at the schools they had been attending; 2) that at least one black high school and one elementary school remain open; 3) that there be a black representative on the school board; and 4) that the administrative leadership of the schools be integrated at the same ratio as the schools. Ultimately, none of these requests would be achieved in the final integration plan.

In the midst of the anxiety-filled days surrounding the move to a unitary school system, local school board elections were held in Greenville. Eight of the 17 board seats were subject to re-election. Two black candidates, Willie T. Smith and Ralph Anderson, ran, as did two females, Sara Manly and Jane Mattison. Turnout for the election was sparse. Six white male incumbents retained their positions, while two additional white males were victorious, thus leaving the board with 17 white males presiding on the board that would oversee the integration of the schools. Both Smith and Manly were elected in later years to serve on the school board.

Long before the era of social media, one of the few public forums available for citizens to speak their minds was the Letters to the Editor section of their local newspaper. In the days following the Fourth Circuit's ruling on integration, *The Greenville News* and the *Greenville Piedmont* expanded their Letters to the Editor section to handle what members of *The Greenville News* staff referred to as an "avalanche of letters protesting the educational atrocity perpetrated upon Greenville County by the Court." Here are a few of the excerpts from the dozens of letters published in *The Greenville News* in the days leading up to the changeover in the schools.

I vow here and now that I will support George Wallace and/or any candidate, local or national, that will assure that they will stand against federal interference in our lives and in local affairs, and will work to return our once great nation to the constitutional republic that it was intended to be.

W.J.M.

January 24, 1970

I am twelve years old and want to express my opinion about integration. I feel it is very unfair. Making a boy or girl walk miles to school where he or she would only have to walk a few blocks is what I mean by unfair.

Mike P.

January 24, 1970

It is my opinion that in some way the communists are involved…they want chaos in our schools and for Negroes and Whites to hate each other. I personally feel that Negroes in the South are being used for some communist purpose.

Faye M.

January 27, 1970

Be not deceived. This is but a first step in getting control of our children out of the hands of parents.

R.B.

January 29, 1970

The Governors of other states who are standing with parents and students against forced integration are earning their reelection in the future and perhaps even the Presidency if the South doesn't lose its right to vote as the next restriction…Even if it takes another 100 years, the education system should remain as it has been. Let the blacks make the transition when they are ready.

Carol H.

January 30, 1970

Will we let six men in Washington take our life, liberty and happiness while our sons, fathers and husbands die in Vietnam? This must be what Mr. Khrushchev had in mind when he said America would be taken without a single shot.

Betty L.

February 4, 1970

Whites and blacks in Greenville had developed a rhythm of peaceful coexistence during the Civil Rights Era. Through the late 1960s, different races checked out books from the same library, rode in the same sections of the city buses and shopped in the same stores. With the integration of schools, young white and black children would spend the better part of their days learning, playing and eating together. Fear and ignorance prevailed in certain circles.

On February 16, one day before the mandated integration of the schools, the following question from a local resident appeared in the Daily Action Line, the front-page public question and answer section of the *Greenville Piedmont*:

> *It is generally understood that social disease is much more prevalent in some races than others...In the total mixing of races in the public schools, what assurance is given the general public that there won't be an outbreak of such diseases as syphilis among young students using the same restrooms and drinking fountains? What can be done to prevent this?*

The *Greenville Piedmont* included only the initials of the local resident who sent in the question and provided a tactful response from the local director of the Greenville County Health Department, who gave assurance that the integration of public schools in Greenville County did not pose a risk of an outbreak of such diseases.

School officials scrambled to flesh out the final details of their integration plan in order to comply with the court-mandated deadline. The objective of their plan was to bring about a total student makeup in each school that mirrored the overall 80-20 white-black mix of the total population of the county. Faculty ratios were targeted for 4-1 in elementary schools and 5-1 in secondary schools. In order to meet this objective, 12,000 (7,000 black and 5,000 white) of the county's 57,000 students would be moved to new schools in the middle of the school year, and 531 teachers were required to accept midterm transfers.

Five all-black high schools existed in Greenville County in 1970: Beck, Bryson, Washington, Lincoln and Sterling. As part of the district's integration plan, Beck and Bryson were converted to junior high schools, and their 1,577 students in grades 10-12 were reassigned to white high schools. Washington High was closed with all of its 600 students in grades seven-12 transferred. Lincoln and Sterling continued in use for the remainder of the school year but were closed the following September and all of their 1,307 students reassigned.

Faculty reassignments were determined based on a matrix of factors that took into consideration such things as years of experience and grades on the National Teacher Exam (NTE). District officials promised there would be "no cuts in pay" or job losses during the transitions. The majority of black principals and coaches were forced to take on assistant roles. Many of the black athletic coaches actually found themselves in limbo during the transition without immediate coaching opportunities at other schools. Remarkably, only 10 teachers resigned during that tumultuous time.

The final plan submitted by the district's board of trustees to the federal courts reiterated multiple times their displeasure over the requirement to carry out the integration plan in the middle of a school year and provided warnings about the impact of the midyear deployment. The following is the summary conclusion of the plan document submitted by the board to the federal court.

The Board of Trustees and the Administration of The School District of Greenville County respectfully submit the foregoing Plan pursuant to the Order of the Fourth Circuit Court of Appeals, dated January 19 and received January 21, 1970.

The Plan when implemented, will clearly establish a unitary system by reason of the following:

(1) Complete desegregation of faculties

(2) Reassignment of pupils to approximate as nearly as possible the ratio presently existing throughout the District

(3) Establishment of a unitary transportation system

Nevertheless, implementation of such a plan during the school year will greatly disrupt the educational process of some 58,000 school children.

Not only would the basic educational program be drastically impaired but great personal and community hardship will be imposed upon the entire county. The psychological impact on students, teachers and citizens of Greenville County will be overwhelming. The difficulties in the administration of such an extreme reorganization are completely inestimable.

The foregoing plan is submitted only to meet the requirements of the Court.

As details of the final plan were unveiled, black leaders sent a list of complaints to the school district. They voiced concerns around the following realties of the final plan: No black coach had been selected to serve as a head coach of football or baseball in the senior high schools; no black person had been placed in a senior high school as a band director; and no black principal had been placed as a principal in a senior high school. The communication concluded with the following admonition:

> *The process of eliminating dualism can and should be a humanizing one in which suspicions and feelings of hostility are minimized and feelings of mutually common trust can flourish.*

———————

No one felt the impact of forced integration more than the residents of Greenville's Nicholtown community. Beck High was set to be closed and subsequently converted to an integrated junior high. Nicholtown Elementary was to be established as a combined sixth-grade school for whites and blacks.

Nicholtown's schools and churches served as hubs for community activities. School athletic events, talent shows and plays at Beck and Nicholtown Elementary were far more than just school functions. They represented community with families walking short distances to attend and hanging around long after the events ended to enjoy fellowship with their neighbors and friends.

Beck High School was built on 26 acres in the Green Forest Park area of Greenville, off Pleasantburg Drive (S.C. Highway 291) near Greenville's first shopping mall, McAlister Square. The school was established to bring relief to Sterling High School, which had been operating on double and triple shifts to serve the growing needs of black students in Greenville. It was named in honor of a distinguished local black educator, Joseph E. Beck, who spent 21 years as the principal at Sterling High.

Beck was constructed at a cost of $1.6 million and opened to students in August of 1965. The physical plant consisted of 40 classrooms, a 600-seat auditorium and a 1,600-seat gymnasium. The school colors were black and gold, and its mascot was the Panther. It was built to serve 1,000 students, however enrollment typically exceeded 1,500 in grades seven-12. More than two-thirds of Beck's students came from families earning less than $2,000 per year; this earned the school a Title I designation. The faculty consisted of 56 teachers, including 11 white faculty members.

The student council at Beck adopted a motto of "Service, Simplicity and Sincerity." Beck's 120-piece "high-stepping" marching band brought energy to Friday night football games, and they typically stole the show at the annual Greenville Christmas Parade. The school's athletic teams excelled, especially the boys basketball team, which captured the 3A championship in the state's black league in 1969.

The first principal at Beck was Lemmon A. Stephenson. In his book, *Three Mountains: An Educator's Adventure Through Destiny*, he described the brief but impressive history of Beck Junior and Senior High School:

> *Beck's history is relatively short, having experienced only four years of operation, but the advances the school made in its educational program and in the programs of the district and the state in such short time were remarkable...In 1969, Beck was honored with one of the most dynamic, aggressive, dedicated, effective, and courageous 56-member teaching and administrative staff the*

world has ever known…Our Beck High School mission was clear, precise, and saturated with an undeniable and compelling drive to delivering the best possible educational and support services to the black community group farthest down on the ladder of respectability, acceptance and honor. It was imperative that we instill into the hearts and minds of each Beck student the invaluable importance of hard work, responsibility, dignity, pride, respect for the rights of others, self-worth, and to hate ignorance, backwardness, stupidity, and all forms of complacency. Our students were never to allow themselves to become satisfied until they had achieved the highest possible goals and honors that their mental and physical capabilities would allow.

In February of 1970, Nicholtown resident Doris Sherman Jones was four months away from graduating from Beck High School. Rumors about the district's plans to convert Beck into an integrated junior high filled the hallways of her school and caused much anxiety and fear among students and faculty.

"I was extremely despondent when I heard about the changes. I felt as though all African-American students were being short-changed," Doris recalled nearly five decades after the decision was rendered that would prohibit her from graduating from Beck. "The feeling of being an African-American youth at this time was one of powerlessness."

Doris still resides in Nicholtown and lives among daily reminders of the hurtful impact of the desegregation of Greenville County schools.

"We felt as though everything we strived to be was being taken from us," she said. "People were making decisions to send us here and there, and it felt as though they didn't really care how we felt. We loved that school. It was so near and dear to us.

"Beck was a great school in a great neighborhood. We had a wonderful staff and faculty," Doris remembered. "We weren't funded like the white schools, and we had to scrape together many secondhand books and hold fundraisers to try to provide the support that we needed."

Once a decision was reached on what schools would be closed or restructured, school district maintenance personnel began to spruce up the facilities at black schools that had been neglected over the years. It was one of the post-Circuit Court ruling cosmetic improvements at Beck that sparked Doris to passionately take up her pen and voice her heartfelt frustration to *The Greenville News*. The following letter to the editor from Doris was published on February 12, 1970, only five days before Doris and many of her fellow Beck classmates were bused to other local predominantly white high schools:

Beck High Gets Green Carpet

For many weeks now things have been happening at many schools for many different reasons. Here is one incident that occurred at Beck High this week:

Monday morning while arriving at Beck, as I entered the door and began walking up the ramp, I noticed that there was something new and lively about the ramp. From the beginning to the end, the workers laid a pretty green carpet, fit for a king. Then as I walked on, I became very sad and hurt. I remembered the five years I had traveled day in and day out on this ramp. I remembered how terrible it appeared to the students and sometimes I would be ashamed of the way it looked to others.

But still nothing was done. Simply because this was a predominately black school. We were not granted anything nicer than this shameful concrete walkway with a rubber mat. I felt that because I was born a black student I was left without the things that were rightfully mine.

All of this beautiful green carpet made it quite obvious that it was because of the integration plan, that because many of the white students would be attending Beck and it wouldn't be right for them to have to walk on such a disgraceful walkway.

Now and every day as I enter the door I'll look upon the lovely green carpet and realize that for black students alone this would never have been granted. It was all right for us to walk on the ramp as we have done for five years.

To many of the students at Beck, the carpet will cause a lot of resentment. They will look upon it as an injustice; they will feel deprived of something very precious to them—the rights which they have always fought for and never obtained.

DORIS SHERMAN
Beck High School

Instead of walking a few blocks to school from her home on Chaney Street as she had done for all of her educational years, Doris spent the final months of her senior year of high school rising early to catch a school bus for the four-mile trip to J.L. Mann.

On the day of her high school graduation in June 1971, Doris walked across the stage at Greenville's Memorial Auditorium with her fellow J.L. Mann graduates. Mercifully, she and others who transferred from Beck would be handed a diploma that day that signified she was a graduate of her beloved Joseph E. Beck High School.

After obtaining her master's degree in library science, Doris spent 25 years as the head librarian at Greenville Technical College where she enjoyed helping students advance in their academic pursuits.

———————

Once school desegregation became inevitable, a core group of local leaders and volunteers organized and quickly focused their efforts on preparing for a peaceful transition to a unified school system; they were intent on protecting Greenville's reputation as a progressive and fair-minded community. Area leaders were keenly aware of the negative economic impact that could result if the process resulted in riots, violence and chaos. Etched in their minds were nightly news scenes from other Southern cities such as Little Rock and Birmingham where desegregation of public schools required oversight by significant armed forces. National media attention of that type could significantly harm Greenville, a city that had begun to bill itself in the 1960s as the "Textile Capital of the World."

Dr. M.T. Anderson, superintendent of the schools, made an urgent appeal for community support, stating that they would accept the challenge to "demonstrate to the nation that Greenville could accomplish desegregation with dignity and grace."

In response to public concern, a biracial committee of Greenville citizens was formed to assist the school board with its implementation plan. The 30-person committee was chaired by respected Furman University political science professor Ernest Harrill and included a cross section of prominent and influential Greenvillians including future Governor and U.S. Secretary of Education Richard W. ("Dick") Riley. Rita McKinney, a white student at Wade Hampton High School, and Charles Kilgore, a black student at Greenville High, were added to the committee as ex-officio members. McKinney was an honor student, vice president of the student body and a varsity cheerleader at Wade Hampton. Her father was the editorial page editor at *The Greenville News*. She recalled attending meetings of the committee at the district office.

"I remember as students that we sat off to the side in meetings, but the committee would stop frequently and ask us questions to get our perspective," McKinney said. "I remember it as a time when there was a tremendous volunteer effort underway to make sure that Greenville handled the transition properly."

This citizens' committee launched a campaign around the rally cry, "The Important Thing Is Education." Over 75,000 buttons bearing this slogan were distributed throughout the county. The committee solicited cooperation from key business leaders, many of whom sent personal letters to all their employees requesting the promotion of a peaceful integration of their schools.

A volunteer army was set in motion in Greenville to handle the logistics required by the court's deadline. Businesses volunteered trucks, equipment and personnel to help move desks, chairs, books and other school necessities. Local churches hosted informational meetings on a daily basis to provide forums for discussing the concerns of parents. Members of the Junior League, along with church groups and other organizations, helped form a core group of over 2,000 volunteers to staff telephones and perform routine chores in preparation for the mass transferal of students and teachers. Hearing about some of the substandard conditions at black schools, parents whose children were transferring to those schools went in advance of the February 16 deadline and cleaned bathrooms and painted walls in an effort to bring the schools up to an acceptable level for their children.

The Greenville News provided a service to the community by printing exacting details about the integration plan as well as details on revised bus routes as they were made available by the district. A telephone hotline was established and staffed by volunteers to help quell parents' fears. Daily, the hotline volunteers were peppered with a myriad of questions such as: Will my child receive a quality education in his new school? What is going to happen to our sports teams, band, chorus, etc.? Are kitchens and bathrooms sanitary? Will I get a yearbook this year? Will bus schedules allow for after school activities?

Volunteers did their best to calm the anxious parents, however, many times, they were being asked questions for which there were no immediate or easy answers.

On Friday afternoon, February 13, at 1 p.m., all Greenville County schools were dismissed for the weekend. February 16, 1970, was designated as an administrative workday with the unified Greenville County schools set to re-open on Tuesday morning, February 17. With the exception of a few buses running late, the opening of the integrated public schools on the 17th was executed without a hitch. There was no violence and only one small protest, a small uneventful gathering outside Armstrong Elementary School on White Horse

Road.

Joan McKinney, Rita's older sister, was a young reporter for the *Greenville Piedmont* during this time. On the first morning of school integration, Joan visited an elementary school on Greenville's West Side.

"I remember meeting a white mother of one of the students who was there to volunteer to help with the transition," McKinney recalled. "She made it very clear to me that her primary reason for being there was to make sure that her daughter was safe. It was obvious that she was not a proponent of the plan for desegregation."

McKinney stood beside this volunteer when a bus pulled up filled with young black students arriving for their first day at their new school. As the children stepped off the bus, one little girl got separated from the group and stood terrified and lost in her new environment. McKinney said she watched the white volunteer's maternal instincts take over as she moved toward the young black girl to comfort her and assist her with getting into the school.

"It was in that moment that I said to myself, 'This might just work after all,'" McKinney said.

The early take on the 1970 segregation efforts in Greenville was that it went smoothly and without incident. A sense of community pride filled the chests of local leaders. They had apparently pulled off what many sister communities in the South were unable to accomplish—integration of their public schools without violence or the National Guard.

Major media outlets were complimentary of the small Southern town's peaceful compliance with the law. The "CBS Evening News" hosted by Walter Cronkite presented a statement prepared by Dr. Harrill of the Citizens Committee, who summarized the desegregation of Greenville schools in the following way: "We did what we had to do, but the people have done it with grace and style."

3
Wade Hampton

We must learn to live together as brothers or perish as fools.

Martin Luther King Jr.

Each morning, before he headed to his job as assistant principal at Wade Hampton High School, Brodie Bricker stopped for breakfast at the Boulevard Restaurant, a cozy greasy spoon located a short distance from the high school. He had learned the importance of eating a hearty breakfast from his days of growing up on a farm in central Virginia, an environment where he said, "Six-year-old boys got up at the crack of dawn and knew how to drive a tractor."

On the morning of February 17, 1970, Bricker ordered his usual: two eggs over medium, grits, bacon and toast. Typically, he quickly devoured every morsel on his plate, but that morning, he picked at his food like a finicky 6-year-old hoping his parents would exchange his eggs for a bowl of Fruit Loops. His stomach churned as he contemplated the challenge that lay ahead of him on that cold winter morning.

Bricker was a boyish 23-year-old, a recent graduate of Greenville's Bob Jones University. He spent his first year after college as a history teacher at Wade Hampton, and his winsome personality and ability to connect with students quickly caught the eye of his boss, Principal Dewey Huggins. Bricker became a popular faculty member with a knack for relating to students while still maintaining their utmost respect for his positional authority. Huggins, a true administrator, was most comfortable in his office, away from the confrontations that often occurred regularly on a high school campus. He was smart enough to realize that he needed a man like Bricker on his leadership team.

Over the summer of 1969, Huggins tracked Bricker down at his job at The Wilds, a Christian youth camp in the mountains of Western North Carolina, and offered him the position of assistant principal. Bricker, who had no previous supervisory or administrative experience, was put in charge of student attendance and the disciplinary measures that came along with this responsibility.

Bricker was raised near Mechanicsville, Virginia, by his mother and his grandparents. They instilled in him a disciplined work ethic, farm-boy resourcefulness and a steadfast faith in God. Three black tenants lived on the farm, and Bricker enjoyed a working friendship with them. He joked that one of them named Harvey gave him his "first hit of Amberjack chewing tobacco." As a high schooler, he participated in sports, playing football and track. His high school football coach was Bobby Ross, who later became the head coach at Georgia Tech where he led his team to the college football national championship in 1990.

Bricker learned many life lessons from his grandfather on their central Virginia farm that would shape his life and his career. Daily, his grandfather shared a Bible verse with his grandson before they began their chores. Bricker was 16 when his grandfather passed away in 1962. After high school, he left the farm to attend Bob Jones University, a fundamentalist Christian college in Greenville. He said he went there to "honor his grandfather." At Bob Jones, Bricker began to nurture his own Christian faith and build a foundation for what would become a distinguished 40-year career as an educator and school administrator.

As Bricker sat at the Boulevard Restaurant on that February morning in 1970, he realized nothing in his background had fully prepared him for what he was about to face that morning. After he paid for his half-eaten breakfast, he drove the short distance to the school campus where 300 new black students were about to join an existing student population of 1,800 that was predominately white. Bricker positioned himself at ground zero for what many expected to be a tense and potentially explosive environment as Greenville County schools began their road to compliance with a federally mandated plan for integration.

Despite his youthfulness and feelings of inadequacy, Bricker somehow demonstrated remarkable courage, resourcefulness and leadership in becoming a sustaining force behind the peaceful integration efforts at Wade Hampton High School in 1970.

As the decade of the '50s came to a close, the Greenville County School Board grappled with the issue of a growing suburban population as well as the problem of two aging high schools in the northern part of the county. In September 1959, the board approved the construction of an eighth through 12th-grade school on 33 acres on Pine Knoll Drive, near the intersection of Wade Hampton Boulevard (U.S. Route 29) and North Pleasantburg Drive (S.C. Highway 291). The school would eventually be named Wade Hampton.

J.E. Sirrine Company served as the architectural firm for the $1.9 million project, which included four classroom buildings, a 500-seat cafeteria, a 700-seat auditorium, administrative offices and a gymnasium. In the school's second year, a football stadium and athletic fields were added. The design of the campus was described as "California style," and as all former students would attest, it was not well suited for moving between classes during cold months. Classrooms in the four two-story wings exited into open-air breezeways. The walls of the breezeways were constructed of cinder blocks cut into porous hexagonal patterns that resembled honeycombs. Cold air and rain funneled through the openings in the blocks turning hallways into bone-chilling wind tunnels during winter months.

In its first year of operation, Wade Hampton housed 1,462 students, which immediately made it the largest high school in the county. Initial enrollment came from three existing schools. Greenville High transferred 600 of its underclassmen to relieve overcrowding which had forced them to operate on a dual schedule in the recent years. Paris High, located on the same land as Camp Sevier, a World War I training camp, was closed, and all of its high school age students were reassigned to Wade Hampton. Finally, Taylors High, located on Main Street in the Taylors mill community, was converted into an elementary school with all of its remaining students joining the new enrollees at Wade Hampton.

While under design, the school had been unofficially tabbed "Northside High School," but as the 100th anniversary of the American Civil War approached, it was officially given the name Wade Hampton in honor of Confederate General Wade Hampton III. Hampton was born into an affluent family in Charleston, South Carolina, in 1818. His grandfather fought in the Revolutionary War and the War of 1812 and served as a U.S. senator and congressman. His father, Wade Hampton Jr., interrupted his time as a college student to serve as a staff officer under General Andrew Jackson during the

Battle of New Orleans in 1815. Hampton Jr. also served as a U.S. senator. The wealthy Hampton family operated an extensive plantation where they owned slaves near Columbia and also had substantial land holdings in Mississippi and Louisiana.

Wade Hampton III studied law at the University of South Carolina although he never practiced as an attorney. He worked on the family plantations in Columbia and Mississippi. Following the political footsteps of his father and grandfather, he became active in the Democrat Party, was elected to the S.C. General Assembly in 1852 and served as a state senator from 1858 to 1861. Hampton was considered to be a moderate on the issue of slavery and had opposed secession as a state legislator. In 1861, however, he remained loyal to his state and resigned his senate seat to become an officer in the Confederate Army, marking the beginning of a highly decorated military career.

Hampton organized and helped finance a Confederate military unit that became known as "Hampton's Legion." Despite having no military background, Hampton demonstrated bravery and confidence in battle. His horse-riding skills made him a superb cavalryman. During the war, he was wounded on five different occasions, including the epic three-day Battle of Gettysburg in which he received both saber and gunshot wounds in July 1863. Two of Hampton's sons lost their lives in the battle between the states. Shortly before the end of the war, Hampton received his final military promotion as he was given the rank of lieutenant general.

After the Confederate defeat, Hampton became an opponent of the reconstruction effort and a staunch promoter of the "lost cause" movement, which asserted that slavery was not the main reason for the Civil War and portrayed the Southern war effort as an honorable endeavor designed to preserve the Southern way of life. In sharp contrast to this view, the declaration of secession issued by Hampton's home state of South Carolina in December of 1860 specifically attributes South Carolina's reason for secession to the "increasing hostility on the part of the non-slaveholding states to the institution of slavery."

Hampton was elected as the 77th governor of South Carolina in 1876 after a campaign marked by violence and controversy. Running as a Democrat, he was often accompanied on the campaign trail by an armed and mounted organized group of white supremacists referred to as Red Shirts. Members were known to intimidate black voters and disrupt organized meetings of Republicans. Frequently, they resorted to violence, and it was estimated that 150 blacks were murdered during the tumultuous South Carolina gubernatorial race of 1876. After the votes were cast, there was a series of lengthy disputes, but the state supreme court eventually declared Hampton governor.

Hampton's distinguished military career, along with his long tenure of public service, led him to be one of the most revered South Carolinians of the 19th century. A 15-foot bronze statue of Hampton on his horse stands on the grounds of the State House in Columbia. A marble statue of Hampton is also located in the U.S. Capitol Visitor Center in Washington, D.C. Hampton County in South Carolina is named after him, and 47 towns in the state have streets that bear the name Hampton. Two high schools, one in Greenville and one in Varnville, are named in his honor.

Fittingly, the colors adopted by Greenville's Wade Hampton High were Confederate red and gray, and the school selected the "general" as its mascot. The yearbook was named the *Trevilian* in honor of the

Civil War Battle of Trevilian fought in Virginia in June of 1864, in which General Wade Hampton led the Confederates to a bloody victory over General Philip Sheridan's Union troops. In the early years of the high school, a student dressed as General Hampton, wearing a full Confederate uniform and a long flowing white beard, rode up and down the sideline at Friday night football games saddled atop a

Wade Hampton student dressed as General Wade Hampton at a home football game in the fall of 1961 *(Photo courtesy of the* Trevilian, *1961 Wade Hampton High School yearbook)*

horse. Prior to integration of the school, it was not unusual for the Confederate flag to be waved prominently at pep rallies and sporting events. "Dixie," the *de facto* national anthem of the Confederate states, was played frequently by the school's marching band and pep band. The 1964 *Trevilian* featured a color picture spread across two pages in its opening section that showed the school flagpole in front of the office against a backdrop of a clear blue sky. Flying atop the pole were three flags: the American flag, the state of South Carolina flag and the Confederate flag. For a high school that was so steeped in Southern tradition and culture, problems with school integration appeared inevitable. A majority of the student population at Wade Hampton in 1970 descended from dyed-in-the-wool Southerners whose ancestors likely had fought proudly for the cause of the Confederacy. The name on their school did nothing but feed the deepest sentiments of a Southerner's historical sense of pride.

In 1970, however, Wade Hampton was fast becoming a melting pot of students from a wide variety of cultural backgrounds. As the business community flourished, skilled workers, professionals and a large number of corporate executives were migrating to Greenville from Northern cities. Many of the city's best new suburban housing options were located in the Wade Hampton school district. Greenville had no Catholic high school at the time, and once Catholic students completed junior high, they transferred to the public high schools. The city's Jewish temple was located within Wade Hampton's school zone.

The mere process of trying to establish an 80-20 white-black mix in all the schools was monumental. Staff resources at the district offices were limited, and the responsibility for determining which families would move where fell heavily to the individual school administrators.

"I remember working around the clock with large maps and color-coded push pins," Brodie Bricker recalled of the days leading up to February 17, 1970. "We were down to the wire trying to get as close to the 80-20 ratio as possible. I remember working seven straight days as we got near the end."

Wade Hampton inherited the majority of students from the all-black Washington High School, which was converted into an elementary school. The remaining students needed to get Wade Hampton to the 80-20 mark came primarily from the Nicholtown community where they had been attending Beck High School.

Similar to Greenville County leaders who were determined to make integration a peaceful "non-event," teachers, parents and student leaders at Wade Hampton worked tirelessly to plan for the assimilation of its new black students. A task force comprised of 150 students was assembled and given responsibility for overseeing the welcoming and onboarding of the new pupils.

The task force prepared an array of banners that hung across the campus on the first day of integration. One of the banners read, "The More the Merrier" while another stated, "United We Stand Divided We Fall." Each member of the task force was assigned to escort two of the new students on a personal tour of the school on their first day.

On the morning of Tuesday, February 17, 1970, the new students were ushered into an opening assembly in the school auditorium. A large handmade colorful banner hung the length of one wall and read, "Wade Hampton Generals Need You." Principal Dewey Huggins spoke to the group and said the school "has a tradition that any student who is new here enters with the same privileges and the same rules and regulations that apply to all. We feel that this is a tradition that will not be broken here."

Head Football Coach and Athletic Director Bill Phillips also spoke and welcomed the new students to participate in spring sports and the next year's football team. He said, "We'll give you everything we have, and we hope that you'll give us all that you have."

At one point during the assembly, Washington High Student Body President Alister Dial was brought to the stage to meet his counterpart, Bob Lentz, Wade Hampton's student body president. Lentz crouched at the edge of the stage and extended his hand to Dial. A local photographer captured the symbolic handshake between the two student leaders. Subsequently, the picture was picked up by a national wire service and appeared in the March 2, 1970 issue of *Newsweek*. The following is the opening paragraph of the *Newsweek* story on public school integration in the South that accompanied the picture of Lentz and Dial.

> *There are a few bright spots in this bleak picture. There has been at least modest progress in several major metropolitan areas, Boston and New York among them—though more in the suburbs than the center cities. And even an occasional promising beginning. Just last week in Greenville, S.C., whites at Wade Hampton High School hung out huge welcoming banners, and student government president Bob Lentz met his black opposite number, Alister Dial, with a handshake when some 300 Negro students integrated the school under a court order issued by none other than U.S. Circuit Judge Clement F. Haynsworth. And throughout Dixie, there was a general feeling last week, Southern Congressional successes not withstanding, desegregation could not be easily turned back.*

Wade Hampton Student Body President Bob Lentz shakes hands with Washington High School Student Body President Alister Dial during a welcoming assembly at Wade Hampton High School on February 17, 1970. *(Photo courtesy of the Upcountry History Museum, James Wilson Collection)*

Lentz, in addition to being student body president, was an honor student, a standout halfback on the football team and a member of the wrestling and soccer teams. His family relocated to Greenville from New York.

"We were very naïve and innocent as to what was going on around us," Lentz admitted nearly 50 years after the day Wade Hampton was integrated. "The picture became symbolic for us. I was up on stage, and they brought Alister up, and I shook his hand as someone took the picture."

Consistent with the conflicting sentiments of the day, Lentz said he got differing responses from all over the world after the photo was published. "Some of the letters I received were very encouraging and appreciative. One person even invited me to visit him in England," Lentz recalled. "Others accused me of being a Communist."

On the surface, it appeared that Wade Hampton had pulled off the impossible, a peaceful integration of its campus in the middle of a school year. Other than a couple of buses that arrived late as the drivers learned their new routes, the day went off without a hitch. Former students described the day as "uneventful" and "not a big deal at all," but even with all of the admirable volunteer efforts, welcoming committees, banners and personal escorts, it would have been impossible to completely eradicate any form of racial taunting in a school so steeped in Southern culture. Administrators could not police every hallway, bathroom and locker room.

Black students who were athletes or others who may have been physically able to defend themselves likely had an integration experience at Wade Hampton that differed from others who did not have the physical or social presence to ward off would-be intimidators. At 5'5" and 104 pounds, William Young was an easy target for racial bullying. Young was born and raised on Bigby Street in Nicholtown. He was assigned to attend Wade Hampton in February of 1970, halfway through his junior year at Beck High School. His memories of his days at Wade Hampton are painful.

"I was safe while I was in class, but once class was out, I became a target for whites who didn't want me to be at their school," Young stated. "I routinely got a foot in the back as I walked down the hallway or spit on or slapped in the head."

Young said he came from a family of civil rights advocates; his cousin Doris Wright was one of the famous "Greenville Eight" who entered the all-white Greenville County Public Library on July 16, 1960. The eight students, including the Reverend Jesse Jackson, were arrested for disorderly conduct and taken to jail.

Garnering the courage to return to Wade Hampton each morning was difficult for Young. "I got where I hated school, just hated school," Young said with a lingering dose of bitterness in his voice. "I didn't go to any ball games at Wade Hampton or attend any extracurricular activities. I just wanted to spend as little time as possible with people who didn't want to associate with me. There were some people there who were still fighting the Civil War."

Young said that typically the attacks on him were out in the open. "These folks didn't fear their actions because you could sense they had the support of their parents for what they were doing," he said.

Young entered the U.S. Air Force after graduation from Wade Hampton and then returned to Greenville where he worked most of his career as a computer-aided draftsman. Now retired, the 66-year-old Young lives in Nicholtown and serves as a deacon at the Nicholtown Missionary Baptist Church, one of over a dozen churches that remain active in the Nicholtown neighborhood.

As the Wade Hampton boys basketball team entered the 1969-70 campaign, it was coming off its worst season in school history, winning only seven of 22 games in 1968-69. Coach John Ross had been the head coach since the school began in 1960, and 1968-69 was one of only two losing seasons he had encountered. Only three lettermen returned from the '68-69 team, and Ross was pinning his team's hopes on several new additions from the prior year's successful junior varsity team, which had won the Greenville County "B-team" championship. Before the season opener against Greer,

Ross expressed uncertainty as well as cautious optimism about his team to Bob Ungericht, the high school beat writer for the *Greenville Piedmont.*

"We can't tell yet just what kind of team we'll have," Ross said in the interview. "We've looked real good in preseason workouts, but you have to get that actual game experience to find out just what you have…I think we will have a good representative team and if we continue to improve the way we've shown so far we could have a better club than last year's."

The Generals' final '69-70 roster consisted of 12 players: seniors Donald Wing, Tom Goodman, George Poe, Mel Tate and Barry Foy; juniors Norman MacDonald, Billy Spink, Will McNamara, Paul Myers, Johnny Ayers and Frank Fitzgerald, and sophomore Bobby Estes. Donald Wing, a lanky and versatile 6'5" forward/center and Tom Goodman, a steady 6' forward, served as co-captains. Wing, MacDonald, Spink and Estes made up the nucleus of the starting five, and Ross alternated a variety of players in the fifth spot, attempting to find the combination and chemistry for his team's success. Juniors Paul Myers and Will McNamara, along with Goodman, competed regularly for the fifth starting spot.

The team was an interesting combination of students whose families came to Greenville from several different geographic locations. The majority of the leaders were not native Southerners. Co-Captain Donald Wing's family relocated from to Greenville from Boston when Donald was 10. Both Wing and Co-captain Tom Goodman lived in the suburban neighborhood of Botany Woods and attended grade school together at St. Mary's Catholic School. Goodman's father was Jewish and a native New Yorker who converted to Catholicism after marrying the daughter of Irish Catholic immigrants. The Goodmans were originally from Long Island, New York.

The 1969-70 Wade Hampton boys basketball team is shown prior to the desegregation of Greenville County Schools on February 17, 1970. Pictured are: Front row: Mel Tate (left), Paul Myers, Will McNamara, Donald Wing, Norman MacDonald and Frank Fitzgerald; Back row: Billy Spink (left), George Poe, Johnny Ayers, Bobby Estes, Tom Goodman and Barry Foy. *(Photo courtesy of Kelly Ross)*

Norman MacDonald was born in Scotland and arrived in Greenville as a 5-year-old when his father accepted a position with Bigelow Sanford Carpet and Rug Manufacturers. Billy Spink's parents were from Pennsylvania, and both were graduates of Ivy League schools, his father from Princeton and his mother from the University of Pennsylvania. Senior Paul Myers moved to Greenville from Bedford, Massachusetts, when he was in the eighth grade. Myers, MacDonald and Spink lived in the Rosedale neighborhood, across the street from Botany Woods where Wing and Goodman resided.

The Generals started the season with a 60-50 home victory over the Yellow Jackets from Greer High School. MacDonald, an athletic highly competitive three-sport athlete, and Donald Wing quickly emerged as the team's scoring leaders. In the opening victory, MacDonald scored a team-high 23 points while Wing added 12.

Wade Hampton's celebration over its initial win would be short-lived as the team was soundly defeated the following Tuesday in a physical road game against T.L Hanna in Anderson. The Yellow Jackets featured one of the top guards in the region in Terrell Suit, a future standout at Clemson, who lit up the Generals for 25 points. The Generals also struggled to contain Hanna's 6'7" post player, Barry Isom, who tossed in 20 points.

"This was an eye-opening experience for us," MacDonald said of the Hanna game. "I remember thinking we had better listen to Coach Ross, and we needed to be better prepared for the other team's capabilities."

The Generals returned home and rebounded to defeat Spartanburg's Dorman High, 73-64. Wing hit a number of long-range shots in the game and led Wade Hampton with 22 points while Estes and Spink scored 15 each.

Wade Hampton was 2-1 as it headed into the annual Christmas Tournament at Greenville Memorial Auditorium. The tournament began in 1968 and consisted of eight local high school teams playing three games each over the weekend leading up to the holiday break. It was the brainchild of local athletic directors Slick Moore of Greenville and Lloyd Kelly of Carolina. Coaches saw the holiday tournament as an excellent way to fine-tune their teams before heading into the throes of their conference schedule.

Wade Hampton's first-round draw for the tourney was archrival Greenville High. The Generals battled the Red Raiders closely for three-fourths of the game and trailed 45-42. The Red Raiders went on a 10-0 fourth-quarter run and eventually outlasted the Generals, 67-54. Greenville was led by its star center, 6'6" Clyde Agnew, who finished the game with 31 points. The first-round loss put the Generals in the losers' bracket, and on consecutive nights, they defeated Carolina and Easley to win the consolation trophy. The Generals were also selected for the sportsmanship award among the eight teams participating.

After the championship game on Saturday night, an awards ceremony was held to present trophies to the various recipients. Paul Myers remembered walking to midcourt with his teammates to receive their consolation award and having a sense of pride for what they had accomplished in winning two of three games and being named as the team that demonstrated the best all-around sportsmanship.

"As we were walking out to the court, Norman MacDonald was beside me, and I said something like, 'Isn't this great,'" Myers recalled. "Norman turned to me and with an angry voice he said, 'No, it's not great. We should have won this thing!'"

The tournament champions were the J.L. Mann Patriots, who possessed what the Generals did not, a dominant big man in the form of 6'10" Butch Taylor. Greenville's Clyde Agnew and Taylor were named tournament co-MVPs. Wade Hampton's Donald Wing was selected to the all-tournament team.

After the holiday break, the Generals lost consecutive games to Greer and Parker. A win over Dorman was followed by a controversial one-point loss to J.L. Mann. The Generals rebounded from the loss and went on a five-game winning streak that included a 56-

53 victory over rival Greenville. Against Greenville, sharp-shooting sophomore guard Bobby Estes led the Generals with 16 points, and the defense held Greenville's Agnew to 12 points. Wade Hampton utilized a sticky zone defense to limit Greenville to six second-half field goals.

An elated Coach Ross told Reese Fant of the *Greenville Piedmont* after their win over Greenville: "I knew we would get better. We are a young team, starting two seniors, two juniors and a sophomore, and we have been coming along."

The Generals lost a second time to nonconference opponent J.L. Mann on February 6, when they were unable to stop Mann's dominant center Taylor, who finished with 26 points and 20 rebounds. They followed that loss with a lopsided 81-55 win over Gaffney on February 10 and were poised to take on league-leading Parker in a crucial region match-up on Friday night, February 13. Entering the game with Wade Hampton, the Golden Tornadoes were clearly the best team in Region II 4A. They boasted a 17-1 record and were undefeated in nine conference games. The Generals stood at 6-2 in conference play and 11-5 overall.

Parker High School opened in 1923 and was built to serve the growing educational needs of Greenville's Westside mill communities. The school was located at 900 Woodside Avenue, in the heart of Greenville's blue-collar mill district. It was named in honor of Thomas F. Parker, the first president of Monaghan Mills. Initially, the school's curriculum emphasized classes such as industrial arts that were designed to propel its graduates into jobs in the nearby textile mills. Athletes at Parker had a history of being hard-nosed and highly competitive.

Visiting teams to Parker could expect a rude welcome and a violent farewell. It was not uncommon for a team's bus to be pelted with rocks as it departed the parking lot at Parker, especially if that team had just defeated the Golden Tornadoes. The school's 50-year-old gymnasium was appropriately given the nickname "The Pit." The court was sunken below a surrounding railed balcony that contained a few rows of permanent bleacher seating on each side. The visitors' locker room was cramped with a couple of wooden benches. As players shed their street clothes, they could hang them on nails protruding from the walls. Showers were notoriously devoid of hot water. The Pit provided a distinct home court advantage.

The 1969-70 Parker basketball team, coached by Bob Winters, was a solid collection of veteran players, many of whom had grown up together playing in the youth textile leagues that served as a feeder system for the sports programs at Parker High. They returned four of five starters from the prior season and were led by 6'3" senior Gary Pittman, considered one of the best all-around players in the state. Entering the Wade Hampton match-up, Parker had the leading offense in the region, averaging nearly 80 points a game. The Generals were the league's leading defensive team, holding opponents to 56 points per game.

Coach Ross knew his team's best chance to defeat Parker would be to control the game's tempo. In practices, the Generals worked on a series of methodical offensive sets designed to keep the ball away from Parker's potent offensive attack. Ross's strategy was working as the Generals held a 36-33 margin with four minutes remaining. Parker mounted a comeback as Kenny Harbin hit consecutive baskets to put the Golden Tornadoes up 39-36 with 2:47 left to play. The Generals' Billy Spink sank a pair of free throws with a minute to go—and that left Wade Hampton trailing by a point.

Parker was unable to convert on two free throws that would have sealed the victory, and Wade Hampton called a timeout to design an inbounds play. Paul Myers was assigned to inbound the ball, and he was given instructions to wait patiently for a series of screens to unfold that should free point guard Billy Spink for an open basket as he broke down the lane. Myers said he got impatient and tossed the ball on the perimeter to Donald Wing before the play fully developed. Wing hurriedly attempted a long jump shot as time was about to expire. As the ball left his hand, Parker's Donald Davis tipped it away, sealing the Golden Tornadoes 39-38 win and sustaining their undefeated conference record.

The loss was symbolic of how close the Generals were to being contenders in the region. They were highly competitive against every team they played but lacked a missing ingredient to propel them to the next level. With the integration of public schools, that was about to change.

Good fortune came to Johnny Ross and the Wade Hampton Generals basketball team through the final emphatic ruling of a federal judge. The forced integration of public schools in Greenville brought Ross the missing components for a championship basketball team. With the closing of Washington and Beck High schools, a collection of talented basketball players made their way to Wade Hampton.

Prior to integration, Ross's team lacked a dominating inside presence. Donald Wing and Will McNamara, both 6'5", fought hard for the Generals around the basket, but neither was a natural post player. Overnight, Ross's team became one of the tallest in the state with the addition of 6'9" Washington High star Horace Anderson and Beck's standout 6'7" center Clyde Mayes. On February 17, 1970, both of these imposing young men became students at Wade Hampton, and the outlook for the basketball team improved dramatically.

Questions arose about the eligibility of the transferring players who had technically already played most of a current season at another school. The South Carolina High School League quickly assessed the issue, and its executive secretary-treasurer, Larry Graves, declared, "Negro transfer basketball players are eligible for their new schools' remaining games."

Due to the proximity of Washington High School, it was clear that the majority of its students including the 6'9" Anderson would matriculate to Wade Hampton. The circumstances around the way Wade Hampton ended up with Mayes, however, remain somewhat of a mystery. Some suspect that it was a process of elimination that led Mayes to Wade Hampton. Greenville High and J.L. Mann already had star black athletes playing the center positions on their basketball teams. Greenville had the 6'6" Clyde Agnew, and Mann featured 6'10" Butch Taylor. Agnew and Taylor had joined Greenville and Mann, respectively, prior to forced integration under the freedom of choice plan. This left the likely candidates to inherit Mayes as Wade Hampton and Parker. A last-minute decision to wait until the beginning of the next school year to integrate Parker left Wade Hampton with the good fortune of welcoming Mayes.

Ross told a reporter for *The Greenville News* in 1981 that during the days leading up to the integration of the public schools, his principal, Dewey Huggins, came to him and told him the lines had been changed. Then, he asked, "How would you like to have Clyde Mayes?" Ross said, "I said 'yes' after I picked myself up off the floor."

Shortly after the new students arrived at Wade Hampton, Ross met individually with each of the potential transfers who had played basketball at their previous schools. Ross offered them all the opportunity to join his Generals squad. Clyde Mayes recalled his meeting with Ross.

"Coach Ross called us all in one by one," Mayes remembered. "He offered us all a chance to play and told us we would have to earn our way. A few of the guys just decided not to play, but I wanted to keep playing basketball."

Five black players decided to move forward and join the Generals: Mayes and his teammate, 6'3" forward James Starks, came from Beck, and Anderson joined his Washington teammates, Willie Allen and Levi Mitchell, a pair of 5'8" guards. With the addition of these players, the Generals' roster would rise to 17. Finding enough uniforms for a squad that large, not to mention finding ample playing time for them, was going to be a challenge. Greenville High added two black transfers to its lineup, and J.L. Mann benefited from the addition of four new players.

Coach Ross discussed the unusual circumstances around the late season additions to his team with the *Greenville Piedmont*:

"I told them they would all get a varsity uniform, and they all would play as much as possible. We have the same situation as the other two schools [Greenville and J.L. Mann] inasmuch as it would be bad to break up our starting combination this late in the season. However, they all will play as much as possible. It will take them a little time to become adjusted to us and us to them, and they understand the situation. I'm very happy to have them, and so are our boys."

When it came time to introduce the new teammates to the existing squad, Ross summoned his current team to the school gymnasium a few days after the school's integration. The players spread out on bleachers on the locker-room side of the gym, and Coach Ross explained that in a few minutes they would get the opportunity to meet their new teammates. He asked for his team's cooperation in welcoming the new arrivals. In what turned out to be a massive understatement, Ross told his team that he believed the addition of these new players would significantly improve their chances of beating Parker and advancing their quest to become a championship caliber team.

Norman MacDonald shared his thoughts about the addition of the new players: "I just remember being glad those guys were joining us. We just wanted to beat Parker, and we knew we had a much better chance with these guys on our team."

After addressing his team, Ross invited the new additions into the gym. The five black athletes entered through a set of double doors on the opposite side of the court. The only sound that could be heard was the clicking of their heels on the wooden gym floor as they walked toward the bleachers still wearing their street shoes.

Four of the five players moved cautiously to a section of unoccupied bleachers, choosing to sit together—separate from their white teammates. The exception was Mayes.

"I remember when Clyde walked across that gym floor like it was yesterday," MacDonald recalled. "He had this big broad smile on his face, and he came over and sat right down between me and Billy Spink."

Best-selling author Malcolm Gladwell wrote *The Tipping Point: How Little Things Can Make a Big Difference*. In the book, Gladwell explained that a tipping point is a magic moment when an idea, trend or social behavior crosses a threshold and tips and spreads like wildfire. He stated that just as a single sick person can start an epidemic of the flu, so too can a small but precisely targeted push cause a fashion trend, the popularity of a new product or a drop in crime rate.

The choice Mayes made to sit in that seat that day was a tipping point and a prelude to a bond that would be formed between a group of young men who put aside their differences in pursuit of a common goal.

4
Johnny

A coach will impact more people in one year than the average person will in an entire lifetime.

Reverend Billy Graham

Edith and Boyd Ross lived with their 2-year-old son T.F. in the Pleasant Hill community of northern Greenville County on a 75-acre farm that had been a part of Edith's family since the early 1800s. The year was 1924, and the annual harvest season was coming to a close. Edith was physically worn out from the endless hours of picking, shucking, canning and storing the output from their extensive gardens. Her 23-year-old body told her that beyond her normal post-harvest weariness, something else just was not right.

She was nauseous and constantly tired and had not felt that way since she was expecting her first son a couple of years earlier. She convinced her husband Boyd to summon the family doctor to their home.

After examining Edith, the doctor assured her that she was not pregnant and that she must be fighting some kind of virus. Accepting of her physician's diagnosis, Edith did what most women of her day did with everyday ailments—she kept about her duties on the farm and prayed that whatever was plaguing her would soon pass.

A few weeks after the doctor's visit and much to everyone's surprise, Edith went into premature labor and delivered a tiny infant son in the back bedroom of their farmhouse. The same country doctor who had told Edith she wasn't pregnant returned to examine the unexpected newborn. This was 30 years prior to the invention of appearance, pulse, grimace, activity and respiratory (APGAR) scores, which predict the health of a newborn, but this country doctor had delivered enough babies to know Edith's tiny child had a slim chance of living through the night. He told the family he did not see a need to treat the baby and offered to return in the morning to validate that the child had passed.

Around the turn of the 20th century, approximately three of every 10 children born in the United States did not live past their first birthday. Parents, particularly those living in rural or isolated areas, were accustomed to the unpredictability and sadness that often accompanied the birth and sudden death of a child.

Edith took an old shoebox from her closet and lined it with the softest fabric she could find. Carefully, she laid her tiny newborn son in the shoebox. That night, she and her husband knelt beside the shoebox and prayed for a miracle.

The next day, their son was squirming in his shoebox/crib fighting for his life. The doctor returned to the house and was shocked to see the baby alive. He said to Edith and Boyd, "It looks like you have a fighter on your hands," and he went ahead and began to treat the baby, cautiously giving the Rosses hope their child may survive. The Rosses named their second son John Wiley. Family and friends would come to know him as Johnny.

Within a few weeks, Johnny was gaining weight and became a very active infant. Edith continued to use the shoebox as a portable bassinet to transport her small son from room to room. She quickly learned that she needed to be careful where she placed the shoebox. On one occasion, Johnny rolled to his side and toppled out of the shoebox and into some ashes from the fire that warmed their home.

Both sides of the Ross family had a long agrarian history. Many in the family were subsistence farmers until the textile mills came along, providing full-time jobs. Even then, most continued to grow crops for their food and maintain a variety of farm animals. Life on the farm was filled with long days of hard work as the Rosses depended on the growing and selling of peaches and other fruits and vegetables for their livelihood.

A series of fishing ponds in the Pleasant Hill community provided much-needed diversions from the daily grind of farming. At these small ponds, Johnny developed a lifelong love affair with fishing, a hobby that later in his professional life would provide an escape from the everyday pressures of teaching and coaching.

Later in Johnny's career at Wade Hampton, he became one of the school's driver's education instructors. Assistant Principal and colleague Brodie Bricker joked that, "Johnny Ross had the only driver's-ed car in Greenville County that had a trailer hitch," which allowed him in the spur of the moment to hook up his small fishing boat and make a quick getaway to a nearby lake or pond.

Johnny grew slowly, and not very much, most likely due in part to his premature birth. By the time he graduated Jordan High School in May of 1942, he stood a diminutive 5'5" and weighed 115 pounds. Despite his size, Johnny excelled as an athlete. He became the star of the high school basketball and track teams. During the summer, he played baseball for local community and mill teams where he was highly regarded as a left-handed pitcher and second baseman.

Johnny became one of the area's best long-distance runners. He once joked in a 1981 newspaper article, "I always did a lot of running because I was so small, I had to run for my life." His prowess as a distance runner may be linked to his childhood passion of fishing. Johnny and his brother and father often fished at Berrys Mill Pond, approximately three miles from their home on Jordan Road. When the three anglers ran out of bait, they sent young Johnny back home for more. He ran as fast as he could across the hilly terrain, six miles round-trip, to ensure he didn't miss out on any of the family's fishing exploits. These frequent bait-fetching runs likely built his stamina and equipped him for a record-setting career as a trackman.

Johnny was consistently a leading scorer on Jordan's basketball team relying on a deadeye two-hand set shot and above-average speed to compensate for his lack of size. Newspaper accounts note several games in which Johnny scored in excess of 20 points for his high school team—totals that were quite remarkable during this era given that most basketball games were relatively low scoring affairs played at a very deliberate pace.

Johnny Ross (left) stands with his 1940-41 Jordan High School basketball teammates and coach. *(Photo courtesy of Kelly Ross)*

Johnny was an excellent student and participated in school plays and other extracurricular activities. As a rising high school senior, he was selected to attend Palmetto Boys State, a prestigious annual gathering of the state's brightest and most promising high school students. Those chosen for the honor meet for a week to learn about government and politics. True to his farming roots, Johnny was also an active member of Future Farmers of America.

After graduation from Jordan High School, Johnny enrolled at Clemson College in 1942 where he majored in horticulture. He was a member of the track team, freshman basketball team and the baseball team. Like that of so many of his peers, Johnny's college experience was interrupted by World War II; he enlisted in the United States Navy after his freshman year.

Johnny rose to the rank of quarter master third class and was assigned to serve on the 492-foot attack-transport ship, the USS *Mendocino*. The *Mendocino* was one of approximately 400 attack-transport ships, referred to by the Navy as APAs, which were constructed for use in World War II. These boats were designed to deliver assault troops and equipment to the site of an amphibious operation as well as to evacuate troops, casualties and prisoners of war. The 20-year-old Ross was on board the *Mendocino's* maiden voyage. The ship was launched in December of 1944 from Norfolk, Virginia, sailed through the Panama Canal and arrived in San Pedro, California, on Christmas Day. The *Mendocino* later carried out transport missions to Okinawa and Guam before being decommissioned at the end of the war in March 1946.

After an honorable discharge from the U.S. Navy in 1946, Johnny returned to Clemson to complete his degree. He rejoined the track team and continued to excel as a distance runner, setting a school

(Left) John W. Ross, Quarter Master Third Class, United States Navy
(Right) Johnny Ross as a member of the Clemson University track team
(Photos courtesy of Kelly Ross)

record in the "two-mile" that stood for many years after his graduation, an impressive feat for a runner of such diminutive stature.

There was an unassuming nature about Johnny that was probably never fully appreciated by those around him because most were completely unaware of his athletic skills and accomplishments. Coach Ross rarely spoke to his players about his own athletic feats. In addition to his record-setting track performances and his success as a basketball and baseball player, he boxed competitively in college and in the Navy. Trophies, medals and plaques from his athletic achievements remained hidden in the attic of the Ross family home in Taylors.

"Dad never really talked about his athletic accomplishments," his son Kelly said. "Things would just come up, usually from others, that made me realize that he was a very good athlete."

One day, Kelly and his dad walked into a local restaurant near downtown Greer, and even though Johnny was in his 80s, a patron quickly recognized him and greeted him from across the room. Kelly recalled the man said, "Johnny Ross, you old son of a gun, you struck me out three times one night in a textile game."

Another incident Kelly recalled was a family trip to visit his sister in Florida. There was a pool table where they were staying, and Kelly said he was amazed at his dad's proficiency with a pool cue in his hands. "He was banking shots and running the table with a skill that I never knew he had," Kelly remembered.

Johnny's first cousin Horace Jones, one of his favorite fishing companions remembered: "Johnny had amazing eye-hand coordination, which made him good at most anything he tried, including pool, ping pong and especially fishing. He could cast a worm into a tea cup."

Former players of Coach Ross at Wade Hampton recall two things that frequently occurred prior to an afternoon practice that illustrate his skill and his humility. Before practice, coaches would compete with each other in a friendly game of H-O-R-S-E. Even into his 50s, Ross was deadly accurate with his set shot and often got the best of his much younger assistants. Before the game of H-O-R-S-E, the gym floor had to be swept to remove a day's worth of dust and dirt. Typically, Ross was on the opposite end of the broom handle meticulously sweeping the 84-foot wooden floor from end to end. Even after a couple of state championships, numerous conference championships and a host of accolades as a coach, Ross demonstrated a rare level of humility infrequently found among highly successful coaches.

Ross's first teaching job out of college in 1949 was at his alma mater, Jordan High (now Blue Ridge High School), where he also coached varsity and JV boys basketball, girls basketball and baseball. Over the next several years, he held a number of different teaching positions at Jordan and Belvue Elementary School while he continued to coach at Jordan. In 1955, he accepted a position at Taylors High to teach and serve as assistant varsity football coach, JV boys basketball coach and golf coach.

One of the most impressive stories from Johnny's coaching career occurred at Taylors in a sport that he himself never played. In 1958, Johnny was asked to take over as the head coach of the varsity football team. In that first season, his Taylors team failed to win a single game stretching a two-season losing streak to 19. Remarkably, the following year Ross's football team finished 7-3-2 and won its conference championship. The incredible turnaround earned Coach Ross and his team numerous accolades and awards.

Senior fullback and linebacker John Carlisle was the most valuable player of that 1959 Taylors football team. He later became a standout football player at The Citadel and eventually was reunited with Coach Ross at Wade Hampton as a fellow teacher and coach. Carlisle remembers Ross as a coach who always had an excellent rapport with his players, calling him a true "players' coach."

Carlisle recalled an incident from his sophomore year when Ross served as an assistant football coach. "We were getting beat really bad at halftime, and our head coach refused to even come in the locker room and talk to us. Johnny came in though and tried to encourage us. As much as any story, that demonstrates the kind of coach he was."

At Taylors High, Ross's life intersected with a recent graduate from Winthrop College in Rock Hill. Barbara Anne Odom, an attractive blonde who was eight years younger than Johnny, came to Taylors as an elementary school teacher in 1956. She immediately caught his eye. When he hesitated to approach her, a fellow single male teacher challenged his shyness. "If you don't ask her out then I am going to," he chided. The competitive prompting gave Johnny the impetus to express his romantic interest to Barbara. They were married in 1957.

The couple settled into a modest lifestyle, surviving on teachers' salaries, meager coaching stipends and a few extra dollars from the selling of fruits and vegetables in the summer.

"I saw their tax returns, and honestly, I am not sure how they made it," Kelly said in reference to his parents' financial status.

The Rosses were blessed with three children—first a daughter they named Cathy—then, second daughter Ann and son Kelly. They purchased their first home in 1959 at 6 Tiffany Drive in Taylors, a one-story brick ranch located nearly equidistant (a little over two miles) from Taylors High and Wade Hampton High, the two schools where Ross spent the majority of his teaching and coaching career.

Shortly after the birth of their first child, the couple joined Taylors First Baptist Church where they remained faithful members for the rest of their lives. After leaving the public school system, Barbara taught kindergarten classes at the church school for nearly 24 years, and Johnny served as a deacon in the church. Johnny's faith was the foundation of his life. Similar to others from his generation, he was sometimes reluctant to speak openly of his faith, preferring to live out his faith through his actions.

"Dad may have not talked a lot about his faith, but you knew where he stood by his actions," Kelly said. "As far back as I can remember, he would study his Sunday school lesson every Saturday evening, and our family was in church every time the doors were open."

In 1960, with the opening of the new Wade Hampton High School, Ross was offered a position that would allow him to teach biology and coach. Initially, he was given the choice to be the head coach of either the football or basketball team. He once told a reporter, "It just didn't make sense to accept the football job since I never played football." He became the head basketball, track and golf coach.

School years for the Ross family were filled with managing teaching schedules and coaching multiple sports, while summers were occupied with the entire family pitching in to work the family farm. Johnny, like so many children of the Great Depression, passed on to his children a strong work ethic. While most kids spent their summer vacations swimming at community pools or just hanging out, the three Ross children spent their summers tilling, sowing, weeding and reaping alongside their parents in their extensive gardens.

The food on the Ross family dinner table came mostly from their farm, and Johnny sold his surplus crops to a local grocer in Taylors. He also enjoyed sharing the abundance of his crops with others. It was common for him to host a preseason watermelon party for his basketball team or to deliver surplus produce to the parents of his players.

Johnny and Barbara remained faithfully married for 37 years until August of 1994 when Barbara died at 60 following a courageous battle with cancer. Earlier that year, Johnny had planted his normal large garden on the farm. After Barbara's passing, he did not return for the harvest. Heartbroken over the loss of his soulmate, Johnny did not return again to the farm as it provided such a painful reminder of the loss of his cherished lifetime companion.

Coach John W. Ross, 1963
(Photo courtesy of Kelly Ross)

Ross's greatest strength as a coach was his strong moral character. His faith gave him an internal code of conduct that guided his actions and allowed him to keep sports in perspective. His conduct on and off the court provided an example for all he coached. Over a 30-year coaching career, he influenced hundreds of student athletes, many of whom likely did not fully appreciate the consistency and strength of his character until they had matured and grown to be adults.

Parents of his players may not have always agreed with his coaching philosophy or the amount of playing time that he extended to their children, but they were grateful for Coach Ross's influence in their sons' lives. Prior to each season, he sent a personal handwritten letter to the parents of each player who made the team offering his assistance to their children throughout the season.

He demanded discipline on and off the court, but he was not heavy-handed about it. He had the ability to express his displeasure with a player's efforts through a piercing look and a short, direct message. There were no fits of uncontrolled anger—the default behavior of so many coaches. He had an intense competitive side that was typically exposed when an official's call didn't go his way, yet he had an undergirding of self-discipline and a strong moral compass that kept him in check. Coach Ross's players did not have to worry about being cursed out because Johnny Ross did not swear.

"One time I was practicing basketball, and Dad heard something slip out of my mouth that shouldn't have," Kelly recalled. "He said, 'Son, if anything makes you that upset to the point that you use those words, you don't need to be doing it.'"

Horace Jones was 18 years younger than his cousin Johnny and was a student at Taylors High where his older cousin coached him on the golf team.

"I remember being proud of him," Horace recalled. "Everybody respected him and looked up to him at Taylors, and it was great to be known as his cousin."

Later in life, Horace and Johnny became inseparable fishing companions, sometimes fishing two or three times a week together. They spent long rides together in the car on their way to various fishing destinations such as Lake Murray, Lake Secession or Lake Hartwell.

Jones, an only child said, "Johnny was truly like the big brother I never had. We would talk about anything and everything. I respected him so much. He was a man of great faith and great character."

As the Wade Hampton basketball team rose to prominence in the early 1970s, the popularity of the game in the state was at an all-time high. At the University of South Carolina, Hall of Fame Coach Frank McGuire had his underground recruiting railroad clicking and led the Gamecocks to national prominence. Native New Yorkers John Roche, Tom Owens, Bobby Cremins and Tom Riker provided the nucleus of a 1969-70 Gamecock team that was ranked preseason number one by The Associated Press. That team went 14-0 in the highly competitive Atlantic Coast Conference and finished the season 25-3, ranking sixth in the final college poll.

At Clemson University, former Army coach and Bobby Knight disciple Tates Locke built a competitive team utilizing several blue-chip recruits. At Furman University, Joe Williams who had led Jacksonville to a Final Four showing, built a powerhouse Southern Conference team.

Basketball goals began to appear in driveways all over the state in record numbers. Wade Hampton was a large Class 4A school, and every aspiring young basketball player wanted to be a part of the Generals basketball program. In a typical year, 70-80 players tried out for 12 precious roster spots on Coach Ross's team.

No job is more painful for a coach than making the cuts necessary to select his final roster. The most challenging aspect usually involves a handful of players who are very close to making the team. The margin of difference in their playing abilities is usually very slim, and ultimately, it requires a difficult judgment call by the coach.

Ross through the years built a system of evaluating players that relied heavily on the opinions of his assistants. Each assistant was given an equal voice in selecting the team, and Ross rarely overruled the majority vote.

Adding to the difficulty of his team's selection in November of 1977 was the fact that Ross's son, Kelly, was a junior and one of dozens of students trying to earn a spot on his dad's varsity team. Kelly had played on the C-team and JV team during his freshman and sophomore years. He was a steady, fundamentally sound player with a legitimate chance to make varsity. He had grown up around the game, and what he lacked in size or natural talent, he made up for with hustle. Throughout the team's summer workouts, Kelly had performed well, even drawing praise from his father.

As final cuts approached, Kelly fell into the category of players who would be on the "bubble" of making the team. All three of Ross's assistants, Lynn Howard, James Andrews and Jim Whitson, voted to keep Kelly on the final roster.

Ross knew that keeping Kelly would mean cutting another player who was also a classmate and a friend of his son. Ross was torn. He knew that putting him on the team would create questions in people's minds about favoritism, and giving him playing time would also be fertile ammunition for Ross's critics. The night before the final cut, he sat down with Kelly and had a difficult father-son conversation.

"He said, 'If I keep you then I will likely have to cut one of your good friends, and you might lose a friendship,'" Kelly said.

Kelly remembered his mother suggesting that he consider going to live with his grandparents for the school year. That would allow him to attend Class 1A Landrum High School where he could likely play varsity basketball. In the end, Kelly and his dad agreed that if he made the team, he would not see a lot of playing time, and it probably was not worth losing a friendship. Also, they wanted to avoid the inevitable tension that comes from having a son play on a team coached by his father. Together, they made the decision that Dad would cut his son from the team.

The next day, Kelly had to face the embarrassment at school of being cut from the team by his father. In the end, he said the ordeal was a "growing experience" for both his dad and him and that he respected the way his dad handled what was probably one of the most difficult decisions of his coaching career. Clearly, that decision further cemented the strong bond between father and son. Some things were just more important than basketball.

The night of the final cuts, the Rosses were having dinner at their home in Taylors when the phone rang. It was the father of one of the boys who did not make the basketball team. The dad was upset and candidly shared his disappointment with Ross, who listened patiently. He ended his diatribe by telling Coach Ross in reference to the decision to cut his son, "Today, you cut a fine young man."

Typically, when receiving calls like these, Ross did not say much because, in reality, there was not much that could be said to ease the frustration of an angry parent in the moment—but this time was different. Ross responded to the dad with these words: "Well, he was not the only fine young man I had to cut today. My own son didn't make the team."

Ross politely ended the call, hung up the phone and returned to his dinner with his wife and three children.

5
Clyde

Clyde Mayes is the best big man we have faced all season long.

David Thompson

February 9, 1975

Six-foot-9-inch, 225-pound Clyde Mayes collapsed his massive and exhausted frame onto an empty cushioned seat on the Furman University basketball team's bench. Playing on consecutive nights in February of 1975 against two of the nation's best college basketball teams, he was off the court for the first time.

Mayes had just been whistled for his fifth foul in a hard-fought contest against the 1974 defending national champion North Carolina State Wolfpack. The four-sided electronic scoreboard hanging above center court at the Charlotte Coliseum showed 48 seconds remaining in the game. The Wolfpack led by a comfortable margin, but the game had been much closer than the final score indicated.

As Mayes wiped his face with a towel, he glanced up and saw a familiar red-shirted opponent wearing the number 44 moving slowly toward him. David Thompson was the most recognizable college basketball player in the country in 1975. The 6'4" Shelby, North Carolina native was leading the nation in scoring, and by season's end, he would receive the coveted Naismith Award, given annually to the top college player in the country.

Less than a year earlier, Thompson appeared on the cover of *Sports Illustrated* in an iconic photo showing him utilizing his superhuman

44-inch vertical jump to lift a basketball above the outstretched hand of UCLA's 6'11" All-American redheaded center Bill Walton. The cover photo was a result of Thompson and his Wolfpack teammates dethroning UCLA from its familiar perch atop the ranks of college basketball. In the semifinals of the 1974 NCAA Championship, NC State defeated the Bruins in double overtime and ended Coach John Wooden's streak of seven consecutive NCAA titles.

Against NC State, Mayes used his muscular body to dominate play around the basket and grabbed a tournament-high 25 rebounds. On offense, Mayes was double-teamed every time he touched the ball but still connected on 10 of 14 shots and finished with 24 points.

Mayes earned the respect of the nation's top player. Thompson didn't wait until time had expired to exchange an obligatory post-game handshake with Mayes. With a break in the action after Mayes fouled out, Thompson made his way over to the Furman bench and extended a hand of congratulations to his worthy opponent. After the game, Thompson told reporters, "Clyde Mayes is the best big man we've faced all season long."

The game between Furman and NC State was part of the 17th annual North-South Doubleheader. The two-day event pitted NC State and UNC against two teams from south of the North Carolina state line. In the North-South's early days, the two opponents were typically fellow Atlantic Coast Conference members, South Carolina and Clemson. By 1975, South Carolina had exited the ACC, and Clemson had no interest in adding games against these two powerhouse basketball schools. Furman from the Southern Conference and Georgia Tech, an independent school at the time, were the alternating opponents for UNC and NC State on the two nights of the 1975 event.

The games were played in the Charlotte Coliseum on East Independence Boulevard, a modern domed structure that opened in 1955 and was home to a variety of sporting, entertainment and civic events. On the evenings of February 7 and 8, 1975, basketball fans from the Carolinas filled every last one of the 11,666 seats in the historic arena. Regardless of the opposition, the two-night affair was the ultimate fan experience for Tar Heel and Wolfpack supporters.

On Friday night, Coach Joe Williams' defending Southern Conference Champion Paladins faced Dean Smith's 11th-ranked UNC Tar Heels. The Paladins led for much of the contest before UNC gained a narrow advantage late in the game. Point guard Phil Ford quarterbacked the Tar Heels' four corner slowdown offense to preserve a five-point victory over Furman. Playing for the UNC team that would later win the 1975 ACC championship were five future NBA performers: Ford, Walter Davis, Mitch Kupchak, Tom LaGarde and John Kuester.

The Atlanta Hawks surprised no one when they made NC State's Thompson the first player selected in the 1975 NBA draft. Thompson spurned the NBA and signed a record-breaking contract with the Denver Nuggets of the American Basketball Association. He would go on to play seven seasons for the Nuggets, who subsequently retired his jersey number, 33. When Michael Jordan was inducted into the Basketball Hall of Fame in 2009, he requested that he be introduced by his childhood hero: David Thompson.

At the end of the 1975 season, Mayes earned his second consecutive Southern Conference Player of the Year honors. A banner hangs from the rafters of Furman's Timmons Arena commemorating the retirement of his collegiate jersey number, 34.

Mayes was selected as the 22nd player overall in the 1975 draft and was the first selection of the Milwaukee Bucks. It was anticipated Mayes would provide the Bucks with much-needed support at the power forward position and become the ideal complement for their superstar center, Kareem Abdul-Jabbar. One of the things that lured Mayes to Milwaukee and away from a competing offer by the ABA was a chance to play with Jabbar, whom he had long considered a personal sports hero. On June 12, 1975, Mayes signed a lucrative multi-year contract with the Bucks. Four days later, Milwaukee traded Jabbar to the Los Angeles Lakers, where he helped the Lakers win five NBA titles.

Mayes spent two years playing in the NBA before taking his game overseas where he enjoyed a successful 12-year professional career playing for teams in Italy, France and Spain before returning home to Greenville.

Clyde Cauthen Mayes Jr. was born on March 17, 1953, at Greenville General Hospital, a few blocks from where his family lived on Dunbar Street. His mother, Edna Mae Mayes, said, "He gave me a time coming into the world," as he weighed in at a plump nine pounds. Clyde inherited his physical girth from his 6'9" father, Clyde Sr.

Before Clyde was 3 years old, his father left the family and moved to New York City, leaving his wife behind to raise Clyde and his two older sisters, Anne and Ruth. During the day, Edna worked as a housekeeper and also worked evenings as a nurse's aide at Greenville General Hospital.

When Clyde was 7, his family purchased a 1,000-square-foot,

three-bedroom, one-bathroom brick home at 500 Glenn Road in Greenville's Nicholtown community. Their new home placed them in proximity of several relatives and close friends who provided Edna, a young single working mom, with a much-needed support system.

Edna remembered fondly the early days of her youngest child. "Clyde was always a helpful little boy. He would do whatever I asked him to do to help me around the house while his sisters were at school. He was just a pleasant little boy to have around," she said.

The Nicholtown community is located in the heart of Greenville, bordered by Pleasantburg Drive, Laurens Road, Cleveland Park and the Reedy River on land that was once held by plantation owner Elisha Green. Green left the majority of his land to his daughter, Dorcas Green. Most of the land in her estate was auctioned off by the Greenville Sheriff's Office in 1869 with the proceeds used to pay off Green's significant debts. Over the next few years, as the land was subsequently sold and resold, a small group consisting mostly of former black slaves purchased sections of the land in an area that is currently known as Nicholtown. Local historians claimed the community derived its name from the fact that back in the days when the area was first settled, "You could buy almost anything for a nickel."

Originally, Nicholtown consisted of a few farmhouses built along dirt roads. In the mid-1920s, its population began to grow significantly, and infrastructure was put into place. Nicholtown ultimately boasted more black homeowners than any other area in Greenville. Many skilled craftsmen lived in the neighborhood, including carpenters, bricklayers, electricians and plumbers, all of whom helped their neighbors build their homes. The neighborhood's residents also included many black professionals, educators, ministers and community leaders.

Nicholtown developed a reputation as a peaceful, close-knit and friendly neighborhood. It was a self-contained community with schools, churches and stores within walking distance. Ladies operated beauty shops out of their homes, and a neighborhood gas station, soda shop and convenience store were owned and operated by residents. Nicholtown Elementary and Beck Junior and Senior High served the educational needs of the children, and over a dozen churches provided spiritual care for the residents. A community center with an outdoor basketball court located in the center of Nicholtown was a gathering spot for youth.

Six days a week, Nicholtown was bustling with activity—slowing down only on Sunday to observe the Sabbath. Morning church services were followed by traditional family dinners. Clyde's favorite Sunday dinner was a plate full of his mother's fried chicken accompanied by macaroni and cheese, collard greens and biscuits. Remembering the appetite of her growing son, Edna laughed and said, "He could eat a whole chicken and a pan of biscuits by himself." Finances were tight in the home where Clyde grew up, but thanks to a hardworking mother, the Mayes family always had food on the table and a warm bed.

The population of Nicholtown increased significantly with the construction of the 204-unit Roosevelt Heights Apartments in 1949 and Fieldcrest Village, a 314-unit public housing project in 1952. Fieldcrest Village was the early childhood home of the Reverend Jesse Jackson, and it was later renamed Jesse Jackson Townhomes.

As desegregation began to occur, blacks became more mobile, and some of the longtime Nicholtown residents moved to other Greenville neighborhoods. Many of its historically owner-occupied homes became rental properties, attracting a more transient population.

Landlords often deferred needed maintenance, and these rental properties quickly became run down.

By the late '60s and early '70s, Nicholtown was a community of contrasts, with many well-kept homes of longtime residents who continued to take great pride in their neighborhood alongside numerous dwellings that were an eyesore and an embarrassment to the community. The proliferation of drug use in the United States also began to have a negative impact on Nicholtown, increasing the crime rate and robbing the neighborhood of much of its historic warmth and charm.

Nicholtown was surrounded by white neighborhoods. On some streets, the homes of whites and blacks were across from each other. Occasionally, children of different races might play street games together, but generally, the whites and blacks around Nicholtown mirrored the culture of the day, keeping to themselves, content to live out the reality of a segregated Southern society. On the back side of Nicholtown, a sturdy fence, constructed of various building materials and standing at least six feet high, ran nearly a quarter of a mile along Nicholtown Avenue. The fence separated Nicholtown from the backyards of homes in the affluent Cleveland Forest neighborhood. The fence remains in existence today and is sometimes referred to by locals as "the wall." It is a symbol of continued separation between parts of Nicholtown and the white community of Greenville.

As a young boy growing up in Greenville, Clyde experienced firsthand the reality of the Jim Crow South. "I remember the first time I went to Woolworth's Department Store on Main Street with my mother. I was probably around 9 or 10," Clyde recalled. "She pointed at the lunch counter and showed me the section of the counter where I was supposed to sit as a black person." Later on, as a young adolescent, Clyde confessed that he and a few of his friends visited Woolworth's lunch counter but refused to sit in the seats assigned for "colored." He said he and his friends were quickly thrown out of the store.

Nicholtown was adjacent to busy Pleasantburg Drive, which was lined with fast food restaurants and retail businesses. Clyde recalled a particular McDonald's on Pleasantburg where employees would routinely tell his friends and him that they were not welcome on the premises. Fortunately, a short distance from McDonald's was a more welcoming locally-owned fast food establishment—Tanner's Big Orange. Clyde said he and his friends were always greeted warmly at Tanner's, and to this day, he visits the business and enjoys their famous Big Orange drinks. Tanner's has been in operation in Greenville for more than 75 years.

While in high school, Mayes inherited a green 1961 Chevrolet Impala from his deceased grandfather. Mayes could run errands for his mother or sisters when needed. On a warm summer night, he could roll down his windows, tune his radio to 1070 on his AM dial (WHYZ) and cruise through the streets of Nicholtown. Once he transferred to Wade Hampton, Clyde used the car to help transport his fellow teammates and Nicholtown residents, Jack Taylor and James Brooks, to and from school and basketball practice. Owning a car brought freedom and independence, but even in the early '70s, freedom for a black citizen of Greenville was not without restrictions.

"A black man in Greenville knew better than to drive at night in the 29605 zip code," Mayes said. Greenville's 29605 zip code encapsulated several of its most historic and affluent neighborhoods and was home to many of the city's wealthiest white families. African-Americans seen driving through that area after hours risked being pulled over and questioned by local authorities. Mayes also said that relatives and friends advised him to stay away from Highway 123 near the Greenville-Pickens Speedway, a location close to where Willie Earle was lynched in 1947. This area conjured up painful memories for many of Greenville's longtime black residents.

Nicholtown was no different than any neighborhood of its type in the '60s and '70s. If you were looking for trouble, you could find it. Rebellious youths formed gangs that protected territorial boundaries within the neighborhood. Mayes recalled being harassed by gang members as a child walking to school, a frightening experience at the time.

In the center of Nicholtown, at the intersection of Dime and Rebecca Streets was Club DeLisa. The one-story brick building was home to a restaurant/grill during the day, serving its popular fried chicken sandwiches and bacon cheeseburgers. When the sun went down, it transformed into an adult nightclub, fraught with all of the typical problems that go along with late-night drinking and partying.

A couple of unfortunate incidents in the late '60s point to the kind of trouble that lurked around Club DeLisa after dark. At approximately 2 a.m. on Sunday, June 18, 1967, just outside the front door of the club, 20-year-old Nicholtown resident Lawrence Lockhart was reportedly wielding a gun and resisting arrest when he was shot and killed by an off-duty police officer. In 1969, 23-year-old Leroy "Hambone" Barber shot and wounded a police officer in a wild shooting spree that took place in the kitchen of Club DeLisa. In 1986, Barber was gunned down in Greenville outside a building owned by Noah Robinson, the half brother of Jesse Jackson. Robinson was charged with ordering the murder of Barber. A hung jury failed to convict Robinson.

Responsible Nicholtown parents warned their children to stay away from Club DeLisa after dark. Edna Mayes was grateful that her son Clyde had a history of steering clear of the negative influences in the neighborhood.

"He knew if he got out of line what would be waiting for him when he got home," Edna said with confidence as she recalled the disciplined upbringing she provided for her son. Clyde also credited his participation in sports, along with his regular church attendance, which helped him occupy his time and stay away from the seedier influences of the neighborhood.

Edna Mayes was a long-serving Sunday school teacher and piano player at Greater Mount Calvary Baptist Church where she and her children attended regularly. In high school, Clyde began dating a classmate who attended Nicholtown Baptist Church, and while this relationship lasted, he would go to church with her. Edna didn't mind so long as her son was in church on Sunday. To this day, Clyde remains faithful in his church attendance, a fact that is most pleasing to his 85-year-old mother.

Mayes was also fortunate to have a number of positive male role models in his life to help fill the void created by his father's absence. His father's brother Claude was more like a dad than an uncle to him. On weekends, Mayes visited Claude, who put the young boy to work in his yard or washing his car. Claude also enjoyed taking Clyde fishing at nearby Lake Hartwell. Claude became his nephew's biggest fan as Clyde began to participate in organized sports.

In the seventh grade, Mayes tried out for the Beck Junior High basketball team as an admittedly "unskilled and clumsy big kid." Mayes was cut from the team, but rather than be discouraged by the setback, he was inspired.

About the time Mayes failed to make his junior high team, his next-door neighbors erected a wooden basketball goal in their dirt-covered backyard. The neighbors' court became home base for the development of a budding young star. If Edna Mayes ever questioned the whereabouts of her son, she typically had to look no farther than next door where Clyde and dozens of other neighborhood youths played basketball all hours of the day and night. Mayes was determined to be ready by the time tryouts came around the following year.

The Reedy River stood between the back entrance of Greenville's Cleveland Street YMCA and Nicholtown. YMCA memberships were a luxury that was not affordable for most Nicholtown families. The Y's three indoor basketball courts were a hotbed of pickup games and naturally drew the interest of Nicholtown's basketball-playing youth. To get to the Y, Nicholtown's youngsters crawled across a large metal sewer pipe that spanned the Reedy. With help from someone already inside the Y, they sneaked through the back doors to join pickup games. On occasion, Mayes was one of them. Today, pedestrian bridges connect Nicholtown residents to the YMCA and the popular Swamp Rabbit Trail.

By the time junior high tryouts came around the next year at Beck, the hours of practice had paid off for Mayes. Standing nearly 6'5" in the eighth grade and with much improved agility and skill, he was a welcome sight for the same coach who had cut him the previous season. The next year as a ninth-grader, Mayes again earned a spot on the junior varsity team at Beck but was quickly promoted to the varsity where his continued development fell under the under the watchful eye of Head Basketball Coach Louie Golden.

1967 Beck High School Junior Varsity Basketball Team;
Clyde Mayes (12) top row
(Photo courtesy of The Panther, *1967 Beck High School yearbook)*

Golden began his teaching and coaching career at Greenville's Sterling High School in 1963 after graduating from Claflin College in Orangeburg. He was the assistant basketball coach at Sterling and eventually became the head football coach.

In 1965, Golden accepted a teaching position at the newly opened Beck High School. He was promised the head football coaching job at Beck but lost out when Golden said, the school's principal "brought in his own guy." Golden was given the head basketball coaching position as a concession. Along with coaching basketball, Golden taught mathematics and served as an assistant football coach and the head track coach. Over the next 37 years, as a head basketball coach at four different Greenville County high schools, Golden amassed 699 victories and won six state championships. He became one of the state's most respected coaches and developed an undisputed reputation as a coach who cared about the young men on his teams.

Given his humble beginnings, Golden's story of success and influence is nothing short of remarkable. He was one of six children in his family raised in rural Calhoun County, South Carolina. Golden's mother worked as a maid earning $15 a week. His father battled alcoholism and was not a consistent financial contributor to the family's well-being.

"My brother and I would get up at 4 a.m. every morning and deliver newspapers, and then on the weekends, we would caddy at the local golf course so we could help my mother put food on the table," Golden recalled.

In 1994, Golden further described the impoverished conditions of his childhood to Rudy Jones from *The Greenville News*:

> *There was no money in my family. We probably would have been a welfare family, but there was no welfare at the time…My daddy would try to farm as a sharecropper. We'd go out into the field and work. At the end of the year, you're supposed to split the profits, but we never had any profits because we had to borrow money from the boss all during the winter to carry us through. When time came for harvest, we didn't ever have any money—and the whole family was out there working in the field.*
>
> *We had a little four-room house. Three of us slept on the same bed. There wasn't enough heat. We had quilts on the bed and got warm from each other and three good quilts.*

Golden's parents did not attend school past the eighth grade but were supportive of their children's academic pursuits in hopes of their gaining a better life than their own. Golden excelled as a student and athlete at John Ford High School in St. Matthews where he played football and basketball while ranking third in his graduating class.

Golden's basketball skills earned him a full scholarship to Claflin. In addition to becoming the leading scorer for the Claflin basketball team, he was an all-conference guard in football and helped Claflin win conference football championships in 1958 and 1960. Golden spent his college summers traveling as far north as Connecticut to work as a dishwasher, busboy, delivery boy and farmhand, doing whatever he could to earn enough money to buy clothes and supplies for his next year of college. Golden was selected to the Claflin College Hall of Fame in 2009.

At Beck, Golden quickly built a basketball powerhouse. After an 11-12 record in his first year, his teams posted a 75-11 record over the next four years. His 1967-68 team made it to the state 3A final for black schools before losing in overtime to Butler High School of Hartsville. The next season, Beck avenged their loss to Butler in the state final and finished its 3A state championship season with a 23-0 record. The following season, Beck appeared headed to repeat as state champs, but Greenville County's school unification plan resulted in the closing of Beck prior to the state playoffs.

Golden said he greatly enjoyed his time at Beck and the advantages that came along with it being a true "neighborhood school."

"If I ever had a problem with a kid, all I had to do was walk down the street to his home and have a talk with his parents," Golden said. "Parents at Beck were very supportive and always would help me out. They would even bring food for our players because they knew some of the kids didn't have good food in their homes."

Golden was blessed with an abundance of talent at Beck, and he said he liked being able to visit the neighborhood playgrounds and check out what kind of players were headed his way. One of the early stars Golden discovered was O'Louis McCullough. The playground exploits of McCullough remain legendary among those who grew up in Nicholtown during the '60s and '70s. McCullough became a key component of Golden's first successful team at Beck, leading the 1966-67 team to a 16-6 record. McCullough is the father of former NBA star and Greenville native Kevin Garnett and the uncle of former UNC Tar Heel standout and NBA player Shammond Williams.

Mayes credits Golden and Assistant Basketball Coach Lonnie Holman for teaching him the fundamentals of the game of basketball and for helping him always maintain a positive attitude. As a coach, Golden was demanding and disciplined, but he had a knack for relating to his players. His hardscrabble background prepared his players and him to deal with many challenges and disappointments that follow a life in athletics.

"Coach Golden taught me mental toughness and really helped me develop my inside game. He was a great leader and role model," Mayes said.

Golden believed in trying to get his team to play the best competition possible to sharpen the skills of his players, even if that meant crossing racial barriers. He developed a friendship with Bob Winters, the young head coach at the all-white Parker High School in the textile mill community of Greenville. In the 1969-70 season, his Parker team was undefeated in Region II 4A and 21-1 overall. They appeared headed toward a deep run in the state playoffs prior to the integration of the public schools. Golden and Winters regularly scheduled scrimmages between their two talented teams, creating rare opportunities for whites and blacks to compete against one another on the basketball court.

"I remember scrimmaging Coach Golden's teams over the Christmas holidays at Parker," Winters recalled. "They were always much better than us and beat us pretty good in those scrimmages."

1969 Beck High School 3A State Championship Team;
Clyde Mayes (51) back row.
(Photo courtesy of The Panther, 1969 Beck High School yearbook)

In Mayes' final year at Beck, the Panthers were 18-1 when their season was interrupted by the county's school integration plan. They scored an average of 83 points a game as opposed to their opponents' 46. Four times during that final season, the Panthers scored more than 100 points, a remarkable feat in a high school game that lasted only 32 minutes and did not employ a shot clock. Mayes recalled that his team relied on all-out full-court pressure defense, rebounding and quick outlet passes to fuel their high-scoring offense. Mayes, a dominating force on the team, averaged 22 points and 26 rebounds per game during the season.

Mayes established his reputation across the Beck campus and Nicholtown community as a premier athlete and one of the most popular students. He utilized his height and sure-handedness as an outstanding receiver on the Beck football team. On the track team, he relied on his natural strength to become its leading shot putter.

While many personal accolades came his way, Mayes was the consummate teammate. He did not draw attention to himself and valued team above individual success. Around the time Mayes was set to graduate from Furman in 1975, Coach Golden shared with *The Greenville News* a remarkable story about Mayes' unselfishness and humility:

> *I remember Clyde Mayes as one of the most unselfish players I've ever coached, and I have used him to motivate other players. When I looked at the box score in the paper the next day, I'd see where he scored only 22 or 25 points in a game. I knew he was doing more scoring than that, so I asked our scorekeeper about it. He told me Clyde had asked him to divide some of his points with the other players who didn't score, even some I knew didn't even get in the game. This is the kind of person he is.*

Physically, Clyde was genetically gifted. His height and naturally muscular frame he says were "God's gift to him." The first time he lifted weights was in college, and yet he was endowed with a natural physical strength that allowed him to excel in sports. On the court, Clyde was a giant, a fierce competitor capable of intimidating any opponent. Off the court, his personality provided a stark contrast.

The words his former teammates use to describe him most frequently are "likeable," "friendly," "soft-spoken," "easygoing" and "gracious."

Doug Williams was a junior at Wade Hampton in 1970. He grew up in an all-white neighborhood not far from the school. He was an avid basketball fan, covered sports for his high school paper and had several friends on the basketball team. Williams heard about Mayes' exploits at Beck and anticipated his transfer to Wade Hampton. He knew that with Clyde's arrival, he would be getting a new classmate and that the basketball team would be adding the post player it desperately needed. Williams did not realize at the time that he would also gain a lifelong friend.

"When the day of school integration arrived, and along with it, many new black students at our school, Clyde stood out—not only because he was so tall, but also because of the people who gathered around him," Williams recalled. "He was clearly a young man who was looked up to and not just in the literal sense. Although Clyde towered above the rest of us and was built like a Greek god, there was nothing intimidating or off-putting about him.

"He was easy to meet, easy to talk with and genuinely interested in getting to know the students at his new school. Clyde and I went from first meeting to fast friends in no time. We have remained close ever since."

Beck High School's final basketball game was played on Friday evening, February 13, 1970. The Greenville County School Board's plan for the forced integration of public schools had been finalized, and the fate of Beck was imminent. The following week, it would become a mixed-race junior high school, and its current high school students would be dispatched to one of three existing white schools.

Beck's 1,600-seat gymnasium was filled to capacity for the final athletic contest of the school's short five-year history. Beck jumped out to a 46-24 halftime lead over its opponent Lincoln High from Spartanburg. In the second half, the Panthers continued to dominate Lincoln, and as they closed in on 100 points, fans rose to their feet and cheered wildly. Beck crossed the century mark with less than a minute remaining to the satisfaction of its adoring and jubilant fans. Mayes scored 20 points and grabbed 33 rebounds in leading his team to a 102-46 win.

Beck's basketball season ended that night. The team finished an abbreviated season with an 18-1 record and was denied a chance to repeat as 3A state champions.

Louie Golden remembers the emotions that followed the final game at Beck. He said, "Everyone was crying—players, fans and all the students."

The Nicholtown community also wept that night. The final basketball game marked the end of a way of life. The school and its athletic teams represented the heart and soul of a proud society. The Beck family would be left with only the memories: memories of football games on cool fall evenings; memories of their high-stepping marching band that had fans dancing in the aisles during halftime shows; memories of Louie Golden's boys dismantling another opponent in a jam-packed gymnasium; memories of spring afternoons when baseball players and track-and-field athletes would be spread all across the athletic fields behind the school.

A three-column article detailing the final game at Beck appeared in *The Greenville News* on Sunday, February 15, 1970. The headline read, "Beck Becomes Just Memory." Beside the article on the same page was a feature photo taken from Friday night's Wade Hampton-Parker basketball game. The photo showed Wade Hampton's Norman MacDonald battling a Parker opponent for a loose ball during the Generals' 39-38 loss to Parker. On the date the article and picture appeared, Mayes and MacDonald had never met. Within a week, they would join forces at Wade Hampton to become the primary architects of a new set of memories.

6
Norman

Prejudice is a learned trait. You are not born prejudiced. You are taught it.

Charles R. Swindoll

Five-year-old Norman MacDonald peered out the window of the Southern Railways passenger car as it rolled into the train depot on West Washington Street in Greenville on a cold February morning in 1958. Greenville was the final destination for Norman and his family on a journey that had begun nearly 4,000 miles away in their hometown of Glasgow, Scotland.

The origin of MacDonald's immigration to America can be traced to a grassy playground in Glasgow in 1935 where 10-year-old Iain MacDonald met 10-year-old Margaret Cooper. Margaret's family had recently moved from London when her father, a sea captain with the British Merchant Marines, was assigned to a new post in Glasgow. Iain and Margaret grew up as childhood friends, living in the same neighborhood and attending school together. Their friendship evolved into "something more" around the time Margaret turned 16.

After graduating high school, Iain began studying to become an attorney, a vocational pursuit that was interrupted by World War II. He enlisted for service in the British Army in 1942 and received an officer's commission. He saw combat duty in India and Burma as part of his service with Third Queen Alexandra's Own Gurkha Rifles and the Argyll Sutherland Highland Regiment. After completing three-and-a-half years of military service, Iain returned home and finished his education at the University of Glasgow and then went to work for a carpet manufacturer. Meanwhile, he continued his courtship of Margaret who was pursuing a career as a teacher. The two childhood friends were married in 1949. Their first child, daughter Frances, was born in 1950.

Shortly after the birth of their daughter, Iain was one of 19 Europeans offered an opportunity to study in the manufacturing field at Syracuse University in the United States. He spent a year apart from his family at Syracuse before returning to Scotland and continuing his work at the carpet manufacturer. Iain and Margaret's first son, Norman, was born in May 1953, and they welcomed a second son, Roderick, in March 1957.

In 1958, Iain responded to an advertisement in the local Glasgow paper that was seeking individuals interested in working in America for the Bigelow-Sanford Carpet Company. Margaret recalled that the ad prompted her husband's curiosity to "see what he was worth."

After a series of interviews and an exploratory trip to the United States, Iain was offered a position at the company's manufacturing plant in Landrum, South Carolina. Iain convinced his wife to pack the family's belongings and leave her parents for what he promised would be only a two-year adventure before they returned to their homeland.

Iain and Margaret, with three children under the age of 8 in tow, flew from Glasgow to New York and then boarded a train for the final leg of their journey into Upstate South Carolina in February 1958.

"As we pulled into the station, I remember seeing the porters starting to handle the bags," MacDonald recalled. "It was the first time in my life I had seen a black man. They were all smiling and seemed so friendly."

The MacDonalds took up temporary residence at the Jack Tar Poinsett Hotel, a landmark 12-story hotel on Main Street. As the family unloaded its belongings in front of the hotel, Norman once again encountered a new race of people.

"Black men dressed in crisp white jackets and sharply creased pants were in the lobby of the hotel waiting to help us," MacDonald said. "Their smiles were so large. I just remember them as a different color but looking so friendly."

The MacDonalds stayed a few days at the hotel before they rented an apartment in Calhoun Towers on Main Street and later moved to a rental home off East North Street. Iain MacDonald was enjoying his new job in Landrum, and in 1960, with their family firmly entrenched in an American way of life, the MacDonalds purchased a 2,000-square-foot brick ranch style home on a third of an acre lot on Rosemary Lane in the newly developed suburban neighborhood of Rosedale.

The MacDonalds were one of the initial families in the neighborhood, which at the time of their purchase, consisted of unpaved dirt roads and very few neighbors. Within a short time, the roads were paved, and they were surrounded by newly constructed homes, many filled with middle-class families from various parts of the country, drawn to Greenville as a result of its thriving business climate.

The process of adapting to the cultures and lifestyle of a new country was filled with changes and surprises for the MacDonalds.

"When they took me to my first American football game," Margaret MacDonald recalled, "after the first bit of action, a bunch of the players started running off the field, and I asked, 'What's wrong with them? Can't they play the whole game?'"

The MacDonalds enrolled their children in Greenville's public schools, and Norman became a first-grade student at Lake Forest Elementary. In Scotland, young boys dressed year-round in short pants and sandals, a tradition the MacDonalds brought with them to the United States.

"When I was in fourth grade, a fifth-grade boy made fun of my shorts," Norman said with a laugh. "After that, I knew it was time for me to get some different clothes."

With each passing month, the MacDonalds became a little more Americanized. Iain was flourishing in his work and ultimately was promoted to the role of plant manager at the Landrum factory. Neighbors and friends grew accustomed to their accents. Their new country of domicile afforded them economic opportunity, a comfortable modern home and a bright future for their children. What began as a two-year adventure had evolved into a permanent commitment.

Not everything in Greenville sat well with the Scottish transplants. Treating others differently as a result of their skin color was a new concept for them. They had little exposure to blacks prior to their move to America, but they had experienced the blending of different races and cultures. During World War II, Iain fought alongside the Gurkhas, native soldiers of India. In Glasgow, immigrants from India and Pakistan lived and worked among the whites.

"Coming here and seeing separate water fountains and separate bathrooms for blacks—it was confusing for me, and I didn't understand it," Margaret MacDonald said.

Norman recalled incidents from his childhood when he saw his parents express their dismay with the practices of the Jim Crow South.

"On Sundays, we would go to the old Greenville Library on Main Street," Norman recalled. "My dad had to explain to me that there was a 'blacks only' library and that blacks were not allowed in the white library. He was shocked, and his feelings came through to me as a 6-year-old boy."

As the Civil Rights Movement began to take hold in Greenville, the owners of a soda shop near the MacDonalds' home elected to close its doors rather than serve blacks. "My parents thought this was the dumbest way to handle the dilemma," Norman recalled.

In 1962, the NAACP filed a suit in protest of blacks not being allowed to use the skating rink or swimming pool in Greenville's Cleveland Park. A federal court ruled that segregated park facilities were unconstitutional. This led to the subsequent closure of the skating rink, and the swimming pool was converted into a marine land home for three sea lions as part of the Greenville Zoo.

"My parents were disgusted with such actions," Norman said. "They were accepting of other cultures, and this was passed on to all three of their children."

―――――――――――

Sports in Scotland consisted of cricket, rugby, soccer, golf and tennis. American football, basketball and baseball were all new to the MacDonalds. Norman recalled staring at baseball box scores in the newspaper as he tried to grasp the intricacies of the sport known as America's pastime, but the strange arrangement of names, numbers and abbreviations simply added to his confusion.

On December 1, 1958, Norman's father took him to the newly constructed Greenville Memorial Auditorium to witness his first college basketball game. It was the opening event for the 6,500-seat downtown auditorium, and it featured a match-up between the Furman Paladins and the West Virginia Mountaineers.

MacDonald said the movements of the game captivated him, even though he didn't understand the rules or the flow of the action. A lanky 6'3" player donning a crew cut and wearing number 44 stood out in his childhood memory. Every time West Virginia needed a big play, the ball was in the hands of this skilled player, who would later earn the nickname "Mr. Clutch."

At age 6, MacDonald's first exposure to the game of basketball was in the presence of Jerry West, one of the greatest players in the history of the game. West scored 29 points in his team's 76-67 win over Furman. The next year, West, as a senior, averaged 29.3 points, 16.5 rebounds and 4.3 assists per game and was a consensus All-American. Over the summer, he teamed with fellow collegiate star Oscar Robertson and led the United States to the gold medal in the 1960 Olympic Games. He spent 14 years with the NBA's Los Angeles Lakers and was voted one of the top 50 players in the history of the NBA. The official NBA logo borrowed his silhouette.

As a young boy, MacDonald was hooked on basketball. His first memories of shooting baskets were of his days on the playground of Lake Forest Elementary School. A neighbor installed a goal in his driveway, and MacDonald remembers spending countless hours honing his shooting skills. "I was there so much, I know I probably was a nuisance to them," MacDonald said.

When Norman was in the fifth grade, a friend invited him to attend a high school game at Wade Hampton.

"I remember walking from a dark parking lot into a brightly lit gym," MacDonald recalled. "The pep band was playing loudly, fans were cheering and the cheerleaders were waving pom-poms—and then the Wade Hampton team came charging out onto the court for warm-ups. I thought it was the greatest thing to see and what a thrill it might be to participate in that someday. I didn't know if I could ever play at that level, but it certainly set me dreaming."

On Sunday afternoons, Norman was glued to the TV watching the NBA game of the week on ABC.

"Elgin Baylor was a slasher with an arsenal of different shots and athletic drives. Jerry West had the classic jump shot. Oscar Robertson was amazing to watch with his moves and court presence," MacDonald said. "Bob Cousy seemed to know where people were going to be and had angle passes that were unbelievable. Sad Sam Jones of the Celtics had a soft jump shot that utilized the bank shot which I studied and tried to copy. Hal Greer was hard-nosed, less athletic but still found a way to get his shot. I studied their moves and shots and would go out to the neighbors' driveway and practice, practice, practice."

Like American sport, American music was a draw for Norman. If he wasn't sharpening his athletic skills, young Norman was most likely listening to top 40 tunes on WQOK, spinning 45 or 33 RPM records, or on Saturdays, watching "American Bandstand." He developed a love for music that would become a lifelong passion. His mother recalled a collection of vinyl records owned by her son that were meticulously labeled, cataloged and cared for.

MacDonald first learned the nuances of American football in his neighborhood. The Perone family lived one street over on Roberta Drive. Vince Perone Sr. was an All-Southern Conference football player at Furman who was transplanted to Greenville from Hackensack, New Jersey, in 1949. After finishing Furman, Perone opened an iconic Italian restaurant and nightclub in Greenville. Vince's two sons, Vince Jr. and Steve, were peers of Norman's and passionate young athletes. The Perones' front yard was large and level, and it became a natural home field for endless games of highly competitive tackle football among the neighborhood youth.

MacDonald was a natural athlete, endowed with speed and agility, which he coupled with an intense competitive spirit and a high intellect, to create the ideal athletic makeup. His natural athleticism most likely came from his mother.

"I realized at a young age that I could run faster than the other girls," Margaret said. At Hillhead High School in Glasgow, as a 16-year-old, Margaret won the overall female athletic competition in the 100-meter dash, the 200-meter run and the high jump and exhibited a proficiency at dribbling in field hockey. Her name was engraved on a prestigious silver cup, which she was allowed to keep for a year.

At Wade Hampton, MacDonald became an all-state performer in football, playing both running back and defensive back. He was captain of the basketball team and one of the state's premier track athletes. As a senior on the Wade Hampton track team, MacDonald posted a time of 9.7 seconds in the 100-yard dash, which was best in the county and only one-tenth of a second shy of the state record. He also competed in the 440-yard dash, the mile relay, the running broad jump and the high jump.

Billy Spink, who grew up in the neighborhood with Norman and eventually became a football and basketball teammate of his at Wade Hampton, summarized the natural athleticism of his friend: "Nor-

Norman MacDonald competes in a relay race for the Wade Hampton track team in 1971. *(Photo courtesy of Norman MacDonald)*

man was a freakish athlete who could do everything well. He was like a modern-day decathlete."

Wade Hampton basketball teammate Barry Foy, who later worked for nearly 40 years in South Carolina and Georgia as a high school coach, said, "Norman was about 6'2", quick and fast and just did a lot of things well. He was a hard-nosed competitor...the kind of kid I would have loved to coach."

John Carlisle spent more than 40 years in high school coaching, including 32 at Eastside High, where he served as head football coach and athletic director. As an assistant at Wade Hampton, Carlisle coached Norman in football and basketball. Carlisle said of MacDonald: "Norman is without a doubt one of the finest athletes I have ever coached."

Summertime created a void of competitive organized sports, and to fill his intense desire to compete, MacDonald rallied the boys in the neighborhood to join the community swim team, which went by the name of Chetsu.

In many ways, Chetsu was the "Bad News Bears" of neighborhood swimming. Their community did not have a large volume of youth, so it was a challenge to a field a competitive team. Their tiny neighborhood pool was less than half the size of a regulation-sized pool, and as Norman recalled, their attire was conspicuously different from most of their opponents.

"All the other teams had those slick Speedo swimsuits," MacDonald said. "We swam in trunks that looked more like boxer shorts."

Neighborhood friend Paul Myers recalled that Norman "recruited" him to join the swim team so they would have enough boys to compete in relay events. Myers said Norman's steadfast belief that they could win a medal convinced him to join the swim team.

The Swim Association Invitational League (SAIL) began in Greenville in 1964 as a way to organize a community-wide swim competition between neighborhoods. What started with four community teams and about 200 swimmers now regularly includes more than 30 teams and nearly 5,000 participants from Greenville County. In its early days, the culmination of the SAIL season was a championship meet held in late August at the Cleveland Street YMCA's Olympic-sized indoor pool. The championship event fell during a time when Norman had already begun workouts for high school football. His coaches were not keen on his swimming once these workouts began, but MacDonald's competitive spirit did not allow him to miss such an opportunity for intense competition.

During the summer between their junior and senior years of high school, MacDonald and Myers prepared for the final SAIL championships of their swimming careers. Myers said the final meet represented several years of preparation. Chetsu's four-person team that competed in the 15-17 age class was comprised of MacDonald, Myers, Steve Vermillion and Frank Huffman. The four boys wanted to go out as champions.

The first event for the boys was the 200-yard medley relay. The team from Chetsu finished a close second to first-place McCarter, which posted a record-setting time of 1:59:9. MacDonald and his teammates had one last chance to win a first-place medal in the final event of the day, the 200-yard freestyle relay. Myers was first off the block, and MacDonald swam the final leg.

"Everyone else had finished swimming, so all the kids and the parents were in the stands. When the gun went off, and I started, the screaming and yelling was so loud, we couldn't hear ourselves talk," Myers recalled. "When Norman dove in the pool, we knew we had a real chance to win, and I believe he took the lead as he made his turn—and sure enough, he pulled it off and led us to victory.

"It was a team effort, but Norman was the hero. All the work he had put into trying to get a relay team together had paid off. In the end, it was his skill that made it happen. If it were not for Norman, we would have never been champions."

Myers played in two state basketball championships at Wade Hampton alongside MacDonald, but he refers to his team's unlikely winning of this race as his "greatest thrill in sports."

As a ninth-grader at Northwood Junior High, MacDonald was allowed to try out for the Wade Hampton JV basketball team. He failed to make the team, but JV Coach John Carlisle was instrumental in helping start a C-team program in the county. MacDonald and several of his friends at Northwood competed on that team and eventually won the Greenville County C-Team Championship in 1968. The next season, MacDonald played for Coach Carlisle's JV team and was instrumental in leading them to the county JV championship.

MacDonald's first participation in organized football was as a ninth- and 10th-grader, playing halfback and defensive back for the Wade Hampton JV team. He would spend his 11th and 12th-grade years as a vital contributor on Coach Bill Phillips' varsity football team.

As a senior, MacDonald earned a spot in the prestigious Shrine Bowl game that pitted the top high school seniors from South Carolina against those from North Carolina. His skill as a two-way performer earned him a football scholarship to Furman University. Despite his success in football, MacDonald admits that basketball was his favorite sport. "I don't think I really had the right aggressive personality for football," he said.

In the midst of Norman's participating in three high school sports, as well as swimming during the summer, Margaret MacDonald never missed one of her son's events. At track meets, she said she would position herself at the finish line so she could "see his face when he ran through the tape."

Referring to the days when Norman was competing in high school sports, she said, "It was the most exciting time of my life."

———————

Margaret MacDonald sits alongside her son Norman in a booth at her favorite breakfast eatery and reminisces about the 61 years she has spent in Greenville. At 95, she is soft spoken and diminutive, yet her words are weighty and impactful.

"He was a delightful little boy with a happy disposition," she said of Norman; "I don't think I have ever seen him get angry."

Asked what was the secret to her family's survival in a new country with a strange culture, she flashes a warm smile and quickly responds with a lingering hint of English accent, "A kind husband and a jolly family."

On the first Sunday of the same month in 1958 that the MacDonalds arrived at the train station in town, *The Greenville News* ran an editorial titled "Tragedy in New York's Mixed Schools." The lengthy piece highlighted a series of violent and negative incidents that occurred in New York City in the wake of the desegregation of its public schools, emphasizing the risks and dangers associated with a unified school system. The opinion voiced by the editors of the paper concluded with the following statement:

> *Those New Yorkers who have sincerely wondered why Southerners have resisted integration of their schools should now have their answer. And whatever it must do to protect its children, both White and Negro, from such tragic developments South Carolina should do.*

The community of Greenville would ultimately be spared from the level of violence and protest that was referenced in the editorial. In the end, it appears that had less to do with organized efforts and far more to do with "delightful little boys" who grew up in homes with parents who taught their children to respect all people, regardless of ethnicity.

7
One Team

It is amazing what you can accomplish if you don't care who gets the credit.

President Harry S. Truman

Coach Johnny Ross sat at a metal desk in the cramped athletic offices at Wade Hampton High pondering the challenge of meshing five new black players with his existing 10 white players two-thirds of the way through the 1969-70 basketball season.

A practical challenge facing Ross was locating five additional uniforms, warm-up suits and gym bags for the new arrivals. Fortunately, two players had dropped off the team during the season and freed a couple of uniforms. Junior Frank Fitzgerald's mother underwent shoulder surgery, and Frank was needed to help in their home while senior George Poe, after being slowed by an early season ankle injury, elected to drop off the team and use his spare time to prepare for the upcoming spring golf season.

Approximately 300 young black men and women were added to Wade Hampton's student body on the morning of Tuesday, February 17, and the basketball team was scheduled to play a home conference game against T.L. Hanna of Anderson that evening. The South Carolina High School League had not yet provided an official ruling on whether the transferred players could participate in winter sports at their new schools, so Wade Hampton's five new players were forced to sit on the bench in their street clothes alongside their new teammates.

Earlier in the season, Hanna had defeated Wade Hampton 75-58 on the road, but the Generals had improved steadily since that loss. With a win, they could replace Hanna as the second-place team in the conference behind league-leading Parker. After a listless first half performance that ended in a 24-24 tie, Ross delivered a spirited message to his team in the Generals' locker room.

"We just stood around in the first half," Ross told the *Greenville Piedmont* after the game. "We were just lucky they stood around with us. When we went in at halftime, we talked things over, and the boys decided to really hustle in the second half. Our boys played like they are supposed to and capable of playing."

The Generals shot 62 percent from the floor in the second half as they rolled to a 68-48 victory. Norman MacDonald led the team with 18 points, and Bobby Estes added 10. Hanna's Terrell Suit led all scorers with 25. The win upped the Generals' record to 12-7 overall and 7-3 in the conference. The game marked the last time in the school's history that its boys basketball team consisted of all white players.

On Thursday, February 19, the South Carolina High School League officially declared that the transferring players were eligible to play in their new school's remaining games, as long as they had not already participated in 20 games during their season. None of the Wade Hampton transfer players had exceeded the 20-game limit.

Two other Greenville County basketball teams benefited from the midyear transfers. Greenville High added Beck's Nixon Allen, a 5'11" junior guard, and Greg Sligh, a 6'2" sophomore forward. J.L. Mann added four seniors from Beck's team: 6'2" Lavanda Sweeny, 6' Barry McCullough, 6'1" William Yeargin and 6' James Cunningham.

Greenville's head coach, Smith Danielson, and J.L. Mann's head coach, Ronnie Moore, faced the same challenge as Ross in trying to merge the new players into their existing teams. In an interview with the *Greenville Piedmont,* all three coaches expressed common concerns about the difficulty of integrating the new players without disrespecting their existing players or upsetting team chemistry.

It was an unprecedented occurrence, and there was no easy answer for how to handle the delicate blending of old and new personnel. Coach Ross decided to consult with his team co-captains, seniors Donald Wing and Tom Goodman.

Sam Walker, an experienced investigative reporter from *The Wall Street Journal,* authored *The Captain Class: The Hidden Force That Creates the World's Greatest Teams,* a 2017 book detailing the significant role that team captains played on many of sports' greatest teams. The book's fundamental findings centered on the premise that "the most critical ingredient in a team that achieves and sustains historic greatness is the character of the player who leads it." Walker described the role of a team captain as follows:

> *The captain is the figure who holds sway over the dressing room by speaking to teammates as a peer, counseling them on and off the field, motivating them, challenging them, protecting them, resolving disputes, enforcing standards, inspiring fear when necessary, and above all setting a tone with words and deeds.*

The backgrounds of the two captains of the Wade Hampton basketball team were not what one might have expected for a school named after a Confederate general. Both Wing and Goodman were Northern transplants and had attended St. Mary's Catholic School through the ninth grade. The Wings relocated to Greenville in 1962 when Ralph Wing accepted a job at the Cryovac Division of W.R. Grace. The Goodmans came to South Carolina in 1965 from Richmond via Long Island when William Goodman, an engineer, went to work at Platt Saco Lowell in Easley. Wing and Goodman lived on the same street, Bridgewater Drive, in the Botany Woods subdivision. They were excellent students, and both eventually became physicians.

Ralph and Gertrude Wing had five sons, the youngest of whom were triplets. On the evening of Wednesday, February 26, 1969, Ralph watched Donald score eight points in a reserve role in the first round of the Region II 4A tournament. The next morning, while driving to work, Ralph swerved to miss a dog crossing the road and lost control of his 1954 candy-apple red Jaguar. His front wheel dipped off the pavement causing the car to flip. Wing was killed in the single-car accident at the age of 48.

Thirty-two years later, while on his way to work, Ralph's son Donald was driving along a curvy stretch of road near his home at The Cliffs community on Glassy Mountain. A dense fog limited visibility, and Wing's car ran off a steep embankment. He died shortly after he arrived at St. Francis Hospital where he worked as an emergency room physician. Donald also was 48 at the time of his death.

"Donald was the kindest most caring human being you would ever meet," his younger brother Jeff recalled. "He was brilliant, sometimes lacking common sense, but incredibly smart. He was fun-loving…always looking for a way to prank you or crack a joke." Jeff added that he frequently practiced basketball on the goal that hung over their carport, and he was an "intensely competitive athlete."

Bobby Estes remembered Wing's lighter side. "He liked to joke and cut up," Estes said of his lanky 6'5" teammate. "He gave everybody a nickname. I remember that he liked to call me 'Steeze' and referred to Mel Tate as 'Meller Propeller,' but when it came time to play, he was an excellent player who had a good jump shot and played tough inside."

Goodman was an undersized forward who had proven to be a capable scorer when given the opportunity. Earlier in the year, he had netted a team-high 20 points in a win over Greenwood. Goodman had worked his way into the fifth starting spot on the team, but with the addition of the new players, he was the most likely candidate to lose his starting position. He was one of five on the team who were members of the National Honor Society.

Donald Wing (34) and Tom Goodman (22)
served as co-captains for the 1970 team.
(Photo courtesy of the Trevilian,
1970 Wade Hampton High School yearbook)

Goodman recalled Coach Ross consulting with him about how to best integrate the new players into the team.

"I told Coach that these guys were really good players and that we should definitely play them," Goodman said. "But I suggested that he not start them initially."

The first practice with the new additions was on Wednesday afternoon after the Hanna game. Varsity practice started immediately after school and typically lasted an hour and a half to two hours. The JV team practiced after the varsity.

Ross and Assistant Coach John Carlisle had only two days to prepare their expanded team for Friday night's home game against Gaffney. Practice ran longer on these two days, leaving a frustrated junior varsity team waiting in the hallway outside the gym. Ross knew that successful integration of the new players carried significance beyond basketball. The JV team would just have to wait.

On the court, the black players had to adapt to a new style of basketball. Mayes and James Starks came from a Beck team that utilized a fast-paced offense and a full-court pressure defense. Horace Anderson, Willie Allen and Levi Mitchell played for a Washington High team that was also accustomed to an up-tempo pace of play. Also, Beck and Washington had previously been archrivals among black schools, and now players from these former rivals found themselves competing alongside each other at Wade Hampton.

Coach Ross's philosophy was centered on patterned offensive sets and a match-up zone defense. He believed in relentless execution of the fundamentals of the game. His practices always included drills to review and reinforce these fundamentals. Recognizing that he also had a strong inside presence with the addition of the 6'7" Mayes and 6'9" Anderson, Ross relentlessly instructed his guards to pass up an

The 1969-70 Wade Hampton boys basketball team after the desegregation of public schools on February 17, 1970.
Bottom row: Coach Johnny Ross (left), Billy Spink, Barry Foy, Bobby Estes, Norman MacDonald, Tom Goodman, Willie Allen and Levi Mitchell; Top row: Mel Tate, Donald Wing, Clyde Mayes, Horace Anderson, Will McNamara, Paul Myers and Johnny Ayers. Not pictured: James Starks
(Photo courtesy of Kelly Ross)

open outside shot in order to get the ball inside for a higher percentage attempt.

Ross was a defense-minded coach, and the Generals were leading the conference in team defense. He was a pioneer in deploying the match-up zone in high school. His match-up had many similarities to the one utilized and made famous by Syracuse's Hall of Fame coach, Jim Boheim.

The match-up zone combines man-to-man with zone principles. Unlike a typical zone where players are asked to cover only a specific area of the court, a match-up zone requires that on-ball defenders stay with the player with the ball until that player passes or shoots. Away from the ball, the match-up resembles help-side man-to-man defense. It is often confusing to opponents as plays designed to attack a typical zone defense are ineffective.

In November 1970, Ross wrote an article called "Match-Up Defense for High School Basketball" that appeared in *Coaching Clinic*, a national publication. In it, he outlined the mechanics of the match-up zone:

> *Match-up is the answer to many defensive problems in high school basketball today...In running our match-up, we use all man-to-man principles as far as weak and strong side areas are concerned. However, we do not send people through with cutters or pickers. We find that we can shift to an overload situation and remain in a basic match-up defense, still with strategic man-to-man principles.*

By tipoff of the Friday game against Gaffney, the Wade Hampton gym was filled to capacity. The facility was fairly typical of high school gyms built in the 1960s, with a dozen rows of pullout bleachers flanking both sides of the wooden court. The bottom row of the bleachers stretched to within a couple of feet of the action. The three-second lanes and the center circle were painted red and trimmed in black and gray. A lone scoreboard hung on the wall near the ceiling at one end of the gym, and it provided little more than the essential information of time and score. Gray pads hung on the wall behind each basket to prevent injuries.

At center court on the far side of the gym was a six-foot folding table that provided workspace for the clock operator, official scorer and public address announcer. On either side of the table, the players and coaches sat on plastic chairs borrowed from the school cafeteria. The gym had an unusual roof design that featured a series of V-shaped valleys and was constantly prone to troublesome leaks. On rainy nights, the gym floor could prove treacherous, especially for visiting teams who lacked any advance knowledge of the locations of the wet spots.

Wade Hampton students prided themselves on school spirit. They turned out in full force for Generals' home games and frequently draped hand-painted banners with messages of encouragement across the cinder block walls of the gym. The students followed the lead of an enthusiastic group of cheerleaders as they stood throughout the game rooting for their team and harassing the visiting team and the officials.

A talented school pep band added to the cozy and noisy atmosphere. As the Generals ran onto the court, the band pumped out the school fight song, an upbeat ditty set to the music of "Hey Look Me Over" from the Broadway play "Hello Dolly." As the band played, the cheerleaders shook their pom-poms to the rhythm of the music while the student body sang to the top of their lungs:

We are the Generals
Generals are we.
We're number one and all of us agree
We've got the spirit that outshines the rest
In every way in work and play Wade Hampton is the best,
And

We're Proud of our honor
Proud of our fame
Proud of our glory and loyal to our name
The red and grey will always say we stand for truth and right
Mighty Generals fight fight fight.

Adhering to the advice he received from team Co-captain Tom Goodman, Coach Ross did not start any of the new players against Gaffney but decided that all of them would receive playing time. No records remain that indicate exactly how long into the game it was before Clyde Mayes ripped off his warm-ups and joined the action, but some of the former players joked that they recall "as soon as the ball was tipped up," Coach Ross yelled for Mayes to check in. Goodman, however, remembers that Mayes and the other additions did not see action until the second half. Regardless of when they entered the game, the inclusion of the black players marked the beginning of a new era in Wade Hampton basketball.

Mayes quickly took control of the game with his rebounding and shot-blocking ability. When Mayes and Anderson were alongside each other under the basket, they were like twin towers dwarfing much smaller opponents and grabbing nearly every errant shot. Wade Hampton held a seven-point lead entering the final quarter, but with Mayes and Anderson entrenched in the action, the Generals erupted for 26 fourth-quarter points and coasted to an 81-55 win over Gaffney.

MacDonald led all scorers with 20 points, and Mayes added 15 in limited playing time. As the game concluded, Generals' faithful were excited as they realized their team had found the missing ingredient it needed to contend for a championship.

The following night, the Generals faced archrival Greenville at the Wade Hampton gym. A January snowstorm had forced the movement of this game to an open Saturday night in February. Since the opening of Wade Hampton in 1960, Greenville had become its natural rival. There was no love lost between the Raiders and the Generals.

A student body fight broke out at the 1963 Wade Hampton-Greenville football game when a Greenville student attempted to steal a Confederate flag held by a Wade Hampton student. The fight led school officials to suspend athletic events between the two schools for a year.

Wade Hampton students hung out at the Clock Drive-In on Wade Hampton Boulevard. Greenville students frequented Como Pete's Drive-In on Augusta Road. If a member of a rival school's team paid an unexpected visit to the other school's drive-in, he risked sparking an all-out "turf war."

The two teams had split a pair of games earlier in the year, and the third match-up featured the first confrontation between Mayes and Greenville's 6'6" Clyde Agnew. As the two post players competed over their high school years, their personal rivalry became known as "The Battle of the Clydes."

Agnew was graceful and talented in every facet of the game. After high school, he became an NAIA Basketball All-American at Newberry College and a member of its athletic hall of fame. He was raised by a single mother and had three older sisters. It appeared that basketball came naturally to Agnew, but by his own admission, he was a reluctant athlete.

"My mother didn't really want me to play sports, and I really didn't have much interest in sports growing up," Agnew said. "I just enjoyed playing on the playground and being a kid."

Under Greenville's freedom of choice plan, Agnew began attending white schools as a seventh-grader at Hughes Junior High. He excelled in the classroom. As a ninth-grader at Hughes, his height caught the attention of the basketball coaches at Greenville High, and they encouraged him to try out for the JV team. After making the team, he proceeded to quit after a couple of weeks of practice.

Finally, as a 10th-grader, Agnew played on Greenville's JV team and began to develop his natural skills and find enjoyment in playing the game. As a junior, he was a slender 6'6". He had an excellent outside shooting touch and a natural instinct for the game. He reflected on his first of several match-ups against "the other Clyde."

"The first time I played against Clyde, I remember being scared to death. I weighed about 185 pounds, and I knew it was going to be tough battling him under the basket. He was already a legend around town."

The JV boys game preceded the varsity game, and by halftime of the JV game, there was not an available seat in the Wade Hampton gym. Once again, Coach Ross elected not to start any of his black players, yet he planned to utilize them more than he had the previous night. The game pitted Mayes against two of his former Beck teammates, Nixon Allen and Greg Sligh, who had joined the Red Raiders after the schools integrated.

The two rivals fought to a 30-30 halftime tie. Once Mayes was inserted into the game, the Wade Hampton student section began to chant in unison, "Our Clyde's better than your Clyde." The personal attack must have inspired Agnew as he overcame his pregame jitters to turn in the most impressive individual performance of the night.

With his size and adept shooting touch, Agnew created problems for the Generals' match-up zone. He torched the Generals for 28 points. In the end, Mayes and the Generals had superior size and depth that enabled them to win 61-59. Mayes finished with 20 points, and Wing added 10 to lead a balanced attack.

A final shot attempt by Agnew that would have tied the game rimmed out; just then, the Wade Hampton students pointed across the court at the Greenville High student section and began singing the chorus from a 1969 Billboard top single from the group Steam:

Na, na, na, na, Na, na, na, na, hey, hey-ey, Goodbye.
Na, na, na, na, Na, na, na, na, hey, hey-ey, Goodbye.

The following week, Wade Hampton faced Gaffney in the opening round of the region tournament at Memorial Auditorium. The Indians were winless in the conference and no match for the reinforced Generals, who cruised to a 75-57 win. MacDonald finished with 18 points, Mayes scored 13 and Estes had 11. Coach Ross played 13 players, including four of his five new black players.

Before the second-round game against T.L. Hanna, Coach Ross reassessed his decision to continue using Mayes as a substitute player. Aside from Mayes' incredible basketball talent, Ross was impressed with his likeability and unselfishness. He believed Mayes had earned the right to become a starter, and for the first time in the school's history, a black player would be on the court for the opening tip of a basketball game when the Generals faced T.L. Hanna in the second round of the region tournament. Co-Captain Tom Goodman quietly accepted his new role as a reserve to make room for Mayes in the starting lineup.

Against Hanna, Mayes and Wing scored 19 points each to lead

the Generals to a 76-69 semifinal win. Taking advantage of the additional playing time, Mayes grabbed 20 rebounds. On the same night, Parker overcame a 38-point performance by Spartanburg's Doug Lowe and won 76-69, setting up a Saturday night region championship game between Wade Hampton and Coach Bob Winters' Golden Tornadoes.

Having beaten Wade Hampton twice in the regular season, Parker had a 12-0 conference record and was 21-1 overall. Given Parker's record, a loss to Wade Hampton would likely not eliminate them from receiving an invitation to the state playoffs, but Wade Hampton needed to defeat the Golden Tornadoes to keep its state championship hopes alive.

In 1967, longtime Parker High Athletic Director Whitey Kendall was in search of a new basketball coach. He called an old friend, Neild Gordon, the head basketball coach at Newberry College, for a recommendation. Gordon was quick to recommend 22-year-old Bob Winters.

Winters, an Ohio native, had played three years for Gordon at Newberry when his coach asked him to forego his senior year as a player and take over the coaching responsibilities of the school's freshman basketball team. Gordon kept Winters on scholarship while he served as the freshman coach. Then, when Gordon became aware of the Parker opportunity, he gave Winters a glowing endorsement.

At age 22, Winters may have been the youngest high school coach in the state in 1967. He was only four years older than some of his first Parker players, yet he quickly established himself as an outstanding young coach. His teams were known for their execution of a full-court zone press and a shuffle offense. His 1969-70 team's only loss prior to the region tournament was to eventual state 3A champion J.L. Mann in the finale of the Greenville Christmas Tournament, a game which Winters said may have turned out differently had his star player, Gary Pittman, not turned his ankle in the second half.

Against Wade Hampton, Parker attempted to disrupt the Generals' offense by deploying its aggressive full-court zone press. Wade Hampton's strategy for breaking the press consisted of point guard Billy Spink passing the ball in the middle of the floor to MacDonald, who in turn would push the ball up court and look for Mayes streaking to the basket. The strategy worked to perfection as MacDonald repeatedly found Mayes for breakaway scores against the press.

After leading by three at the half, Wade Hampton pulled away in the second half to handily defeat Parker 74-60 and capture the Region II 4A tournament championship. Mayes scored 20 points and grabbed a school-record 31 rebounds. Point guard Billy Spink added 13 points, including several clutch free throws in the fourth quarter, and Wing added 12 points. MacDonald finished the game with 10 assists, and his overall floor leadership earned him the most valuable player award for the tournament.

The loss was difficult for Winters to absorb. His team had not received the benefit of any new players after the integration of Greenville County schools. In a post-game interview with *The Greenville News*, Winters voiced his frustration. "I don't see how anyone can expect us to beat three teams," Winters said in reference to the fact that Wade Hampton included players from three different schools. "I don't blame Wade Hampton for what happened, but it just doesn't seem right."

Adding pain to the situation was that Horace Anderson, the 6'9" post player who transferred to Wade Hampton from Washington

High, lived less than a half-mile from Parker High. Winters could only speculate that the more conservative nature and heritage of the Parker community caused school district officials to wait until the following year to integrate Parker High.

At the completion of the season, Winters accepted a position as the assistant basketball coach at the College of Charleston. He continued to coach in college and high school in South Carolina and Ohio for the next 47 years before retiring in the Charleston area where he runs a charter fishing service with his son. Even today, the events surrounding the unification of the Greenville County schools and the effect on his basketball team conjure up painful memories for Winters.

"It was frustrating, and I just felt bad for our kids," Winters reflected. "I don't blame Wade Hampton or Johnny Ross; it was just an unfortunate thing for our kids."

The Generals were headed to the 1970 state tournament as the Region II 4A champions. In the 10-year history of the school, they had been region champions only once (1965). A mixture of students from three different schools had quickly forged into a highly effective single operating unit, but it did not come without a cost. Players who had previously played more significant roles on the team were forced to make sacrifices.

Co-captain Tom Goodman lost his starting position. Will McNamara, a 6'4" back-up junior center, had received significant playing time prior to the arrival of Clyde Mayes and Horace Anderson. Once integration occurred, McNamara was relegated to battling against Mayes in practice while receiving limited playing time in games.

Bobby Estes, a sharp-shooting sophomore guard, was asked to reduce his shots from the outside in order to feed the ball inside to Mayes and Anderson. Prior to integration, Estes had scored in double figures in nine of 18 games and was averaging nearly 10 points a game. After integration, his scoring average dropped to half that.

Barry Foy, a dedicated hardworking senior who had seen a considerable amount of playing time prior to integration, also saw his minutes drastically reduced, as did Paul Myers, a consummate team player who had started several games earlier in the year. Johnny Ayers was a multi-sport athlete who came off the bench to help the Generals to an early season win over archrival Greenville and showed an ability to play effectively when given the chance. Like Foy and Myers, Ayers struggled to gain playing time post integration.

Levi Mitchell and Willie Allen had been starting guards on the 1969-70 Washington High School team alongside Anderson. Their playing time at Wade Hampton was sparse, while Anderson, who was accustomed to playing nearly every minute of every game at Washington High, was relegated to a supporting role.

On Sunday evening prior to the week of the state tourney, Coach Ross attended the 7 p.m. service at Taylors First Baptist Church. During the sermon, his mind drifted to the challenge ahead of his team. He knew its success in the state tourney hinged on the ability to stay focused on the task of winning games without concern for individual achievement. Selfishness was the enemy of team chemistry.

Five new players had joined Ross's team only 10 days earlier. The question he pondered in church was, "Could they possibly come together in such a short time and form a real team?" A chance to win a state championship and a chance to make history lay in the balance.

8
Champions

Talent wins games, but teamwork and intelligence win championships.

Michael Jordan

The 1970 South Carolina 4A high school basketball tournament was held the first weekend in March at Spartanburg High's Dobson Gymnasium. The Spartanburg gym, constructed in 1959, was by far one of the larger high school gyms in the state. It was named in honor of Hubert Ray "Red" Dobson, a legendary Spartanburg High coach who won six state championships in basketball and coached four undefeated football teams during his 19-year tenure at the school from 1927 to 1946.

The building seated approximately 2,000 fans in permanent bench seats that rose up along one side of the court opposite the team benches and scorer's table. A tiled ceiling with recessed fluorescent lighting gave the gym a modern look that contrasted with typical high school gyms of the day that featured exposed steel beams and hanging lights. The baskets were suspended from the ceiling by retractable steel framing.

Eight teams qualified for the 4A state playoffs that took place over three consecutive days. Wade Hampton joined Parker, A.C. Flora (Columbia), Brookland-Cayce (Columbia), Dentsville (Columbia), Edmunds (Sumter), Greenwood and Lancaster in the single-elimination event.

During the week prior to the tournament, Coach Ross was bed-

ridden with a severe case of the flu. Ross handed practice responsibilities over to Assistant Coach John Carlisle and Athletic Director
Bill Phillips. Carlisle was a capable assistant, but by his own admission, he was "a football guy coaching basketball."

Phillips was an athletic legend in the Greenville area having played
football, basketball and baseball at Greenville High before becoming
an All-Southern Conference catcher at Furman University. Phillips
was also well known throughout the area's textile baseball leagues
and was invited twice to attend spring training with the American
League's Philadelphia Athletics. After a stint in the military, he returned to Greenville High in 1955 as a teacher and a coach and eventually became the school's head basketball and baseball coach while
also serving as an assistant football coach under legendary head
coach Slick Moore. Phillips' Red Raider basketball teams had won
three state championships.

Phillips was named head basketball coach at Greenville in 1959,
the year prior to Ross's becoming the head coach at Wade Hampton.
For the next nine years, the two coached against each other on the
basketball court with Phillips' Red Raiders winning 12 of their 17
head-to-head match-ups. Off the court, they developed a respectful
friendship.

In 1969, Phillips joined Ross on the Generals' coaching staff when
he became the athletic director and head football and baseball coach
at Wade Hampton. During the week of preparation for the 1970
state basketball tourney, the ailing Coach Ross was fortunate to have
Coach Phillips available to assist with his team's preparation. With
Ross providing counsel from his sickbed, Phillips and Carlisle prepared the Generals for a run at the state title.

The Generals also benefited from some additional coaching exper-

148

tise during this time. After the closing of Beck High School, Coach Louie Golden waited for his next coaching and teaching assignment. Golden was a skilled coach without a team, so he volunteered to assist Wade Hampton during postseason play. Norman MacDonald remembered getting some helpful personal instruction from Golden at a practice session prior to the state tournament, and Bobby Estes recalled a detailed scouting report that Golden provided on Wade Hampton's first opponent in the state tournament, A.C. Flora.

The A.C. Flora Falcons were the defending state 4A champs and had a 20-2 overall record. Along with Wade Hampton, they were viewed as the pre-tournament favorites. Flora's head coach, Cy Szakacsi, had been a high school coach since graduating from the University of South Carolina in 1951 and had won three state basketball titles.

Louie Golden's scouting report revealed that stopping Flora's talented backcourt star Al Flowers would be key. Flowers averaged 24 points per game and had scored 34 in the conference championship game the previous Saturday. The defensive responsibility for shutting down Flowers fell to Wade Hampton's guards Billy Spink and Bobby Estes.

As the 8:45 p.m. game time approached that Thursday, Coach Ross was still weak from his week-long bout with the flu, but there was no way he would miss the opportunity to coach his team in the state tournament. Since he began his coaching career nearly 20 years earlier, he had dreamed of an opportunity to lead a team to a state championship. Ross was still running a low-grade fever on the night of the game, and he did his best to not get close to any of his players as he delivered his pregame instructions in the Generals' locker room.

Prior to the tip-off of each game, every player was introduced over the public address system. The lights in the gym were dimmed, and a spotlight shined on center court. When a player's name was called, he ran to the spotlight and joined his teammates amid applause from fans. Halfway through the introduction of the Generals' lineup, the announcer called out, "Number 43, Junior Will McNamara."

"I remember standing there in the spotlight waiting for Will to join us," Norman MacDonald said. "We waited and we waited...finally we realized that Will had tripped in the darkness on his run from the bench and slid right past us in the spotlight. Only Will McNamara could have done that. He could make us all laugh." It was a needed moment of levity that helped ease the tension of playing in the state tournament.

Wade Hampton led Flora by six at halftime before Mayes ignited an explosive third quarter that saw the Generals outscore their opponents 27-10 and go on to take a surprisingly easy 78-48 win. The Generals' defense held Flora's standout guard Flowers to 15 points in the game. The headline in *The State* the next morning aptly summed up the game, "Generals Destroy Flora."

Mayes finished with 20 points, while Horace Anderson came off the bench to score 12 points and help Mayes dominate around the basket. Tom Goodman substituted for MacDonald who was plagued with early foul trouble and contributed 11 points, as did Billy Spink, who made 11 of 12 free-throw attempts.

Anderson was used sparingly in his first three games after his transfer from Washington High. He recalled hearing chants from some of his former Washington High classmates encouraging Ross to put him in the game. He was the star of Washington High's team, but he was relegated to a reserve role. Off the court, Anderson was quiet and reserved. On the court, he was a fierce defender and re-bounder.

Anderson recalled a conversation he had with Coach Ross in which Ross admitted that Anderson probably deserved to be a start-er, but he said Ross told him he owed it to the players who had been together all year to keep them in the starting lineup. In the state tour-nament, Ross began to utilize Anderson more, and his performance was key in the Generals' dominant postseason play. With Anderson inserted in the lineup, the Generals' front line stood 6'7" (Mayes), 6'7" (Anderson) and 6'5" (Donald Wing) and afforded them a size-able advantage over opponents.

Lancaster defeated Brookland-Cayce 57-51 in its opening game to earn the opportunity to play Wade Hampton in Friday night's semi-final round. Lancaster was the surprise entry in the tournament as it had a 7-16 regular season record yet made the state tourney after a strong showing in its conference tournament. Dentsville eliminated Parker in its first-round match-up behind a 41-point performance by talented guard David Havird. Dentsville's semifinal opponent was Edmunds, which had defeated Greenwood in its opener.

Against Lancaster, Mayes once again controlled the game from inside, scoring 19 points and grabbing 20 rebounds in leading Wade Hampton to a 76-46 win. MacDonald added 13, Anderson scored 10 and Spink had nine in the Generals' second consecutive 30-point victory.

With Anderson and Mayes playing much of the game alongside each other, Wade Hampton outrebounded Lancaster 48-24. The Generals shot 49 percent from the field and 85 percent from the free-throw line while holding Lancaster to 33 percent shooting from the field. Wade Hampton went on a 16-0 run early in the fourth quarter for a comfortable 65-34 lead, which allowed Coach Ross to clear his bench with three minutes to play.

Edmunds High of Sumter defeated Dentsville 56-53 in the other semifinal match-up to set up the championship game against Wade Hampton on Saturday night.

The state tourney weekend coincided with the popular Atlantic Coast Conference collegiate basketball tournament being held 75 miles northeast of Spartanburg in the Charlotte Coliseum. The favorite to win the 1970 tourney was Frank McGuire's South Carolina Gamecock team, which was 16-0 in conference play and 22-2 overall. The Gamecocks had begun the season ranked first in the nation by The Associated Press.

In Friday evening's semifinal game, South Carolina faced Wake Forest. A security guard at Dobson Gymnasium sitting on a concrete runway above the bleachers had brought a 24-inch black-and-white TV complete with rabbit ear antennas in order to watch the tournament action. As the Wade Hampton game became a lopsided affair, a steady stream of fans made their way to the runway on the upper concourse to catch glimpses of the USC-Wake Forest game on the small screen.

The Gamecocks' All-American guard John Roche twisted his ankle while driving for a layup, and, with his injury, the Gamecocks saw their chances of a deep run in the NCAA Tournament diminished. The fans gathered around the TV and watched as Roche lay on the Charlotte Coliseum floor writhing in pain while the high school action continued on the court at Dobson Gymnasium.

The Gamecocks defeated Wake Forest, but the next night, they lost in double overtime to NC State, a team they had beaten twice during the regular season. Roche attempted to play on his injured ankle but was ineffective, making only four of his 17 shot attempts and scoring nine points against the Wolfpack.

The only way for an ACC team to receive a bid to the NCAA tournament in 1970 was to win the conference tournament, so South Carolina's dream season ended on that March night in Charlotte. The Gamecocks finished ranked sixth in the final Associated Press poll. One basketball team's dream died on that Saturday evening, and another's was about to be fulfilled.

The championship game was set for 8:30 p.m. on Saturday in Spartanburg and was preceded by a consolation game between Dentsville and Lancaster. The Wade Hampton players met at their normal loading spot, the athletic parking lot outside Wade Hampton's gym at 5 p.m. Students commonly referred to this lot as the "jock lot."

Coach Carlisle also served as the team's regular bus driver. An incident earlier in the year had given the boys a confident respect for their assistant coach and bus driver. After a narrow defeat to Parker, the team's bus sat idling in the parking lot as everyone was waiting for Coach Ross to join them for the ride home. The players were sitting quietly, downtrodden from their defeat, when suddenly, shattered glass flew through the bus.

A group of rowdy Parker students began pelting the bus with rocks. Several of the windows were shattered, and one player, Paul

Myers, was cut. As the rocks began to hit the bus, Coach Carlisle, an ex-Citadel football star, threw open the bus door and began to chase the attackers.

"He was gone for about five minutes, and I don't know if he caught them or not," Norman MacDonald recalled. "I just remember that we were all very impressed with Coach Carlisle's fearlessness."

The team rode in silence during the 42-mile trip to Spartanburg High, well aware of the significance of the task at hand. The players entered the gym through a back entrance and found their way to an open section of bleachers to watch the consolation match-up. With approximately four minutes left in the third quarter of preliminary game, the Generals went to their locker room to dress. The Generals were the visiting team and were assigned the PE locker room normally used by the girls. They hung their clothes in open lockers and put their wallets and watches in a secure box that the team manager kept with him on the bench during the game.

Wade Hampton dressed in its traveling uniforms that featured red satin finished pants and shirts trimmed in white and gray. "Generals" was stitched in white letters across the front of the jerseys, and their numbers were displayed prominently on the front and back. The pants fastened in the front with a silver belt buckle. Players wore matching knee-high red socks and white canvas Chuck Taylor Converse high tops.

Coach Ross and Coach Carlisle huddled in a corner of the room and spoke quietly to each other as the players dressed. The fully dressed team sat silently along a couple of wooden benches in the sparsely decorated locker room and waited for final instructions. The silence was broken by the friction of Coach Ross's leather-soled shoes sliding across the concrete floor.

Ross was not prone to give highly emotional pregame speeches. He spoke to his team as if he were talking to his family around the dinner table. He told them to keep doing the things that had gotten them to that point: playing hard-nosed defense, rebounding and getting the ball inside to their big men for the high percentage shot. He reminded them not to panic against the press but to focus on getting the ball into the middle of the court to avoid being trapped in the corners.

Their opponent, Edmunds High of Sumter, had a 20-5 record and was led by a pair of talented guards, Mike Heriot and Ronnie Motley, along with 6'5" center Tip Kilby. Together, these three players had scored 80 percent of their team's points in the first two games of the state tournament. Edmunds was coached by first-year head coach Jimmy Boykin. Earlier in the school year, the school's football team had defeated the Gaffney Indians to win the state 4A championship.

It would not be until the next fall that Edmunds and Sumter's all-black Lincoln High were combined to form what is now called Sumter High School. Edmunds had a handful of black students already enrolled in the school in 1970, including Mike Heriot, the lone black member of the basketball team.

Ross instructed his team to center their defensive focus on the three key Edmunds players. The Generals had watched Edmunds defeat Dentsville the night before, and they had a clear understanding of the skills and tendencies of these three. The Generals planned to start in their match-up zone but would move to a man-to-man at some point in the game. Ross gave out the individual defensive match-ups to his starting five of Mayes, MacDonald, Estes, Spink and Wing.

Ross also told his players to push the ball up the court quickly when the opportunity presented itself as Edmunds had played only one substitute in the previous two games, and he believed the Generals' depth would be an advantage toward the end of the game.

At the conclusion of his pregame talk, Coach Ross asked his team to do what every team he had ever coached did prior to a game. The players circled up, dropped to one knee, extended an arm and stacked their hands together. With Coach Ross leading, they began to recite in unison the Lord's Prayer.

Our Father, who art in heaven,
Hallowed be Thy name.
Thy kingdom come,
Thy will be done in earth,
As it is in heaven.
Give us this day our daily bread.
And forgive us our trespasses,
As we forgive those who trespass against us.
And lead us not into temptation,
But deliver us from evil.
For thine is the kingdom and the power and the glory,
Forever and ever.
Amen

At the conclusion of the prayer, the team waited for the signal from its manager that the consolation game had ended before it burst through the locker-room door and onto the court. The Generals were greeted by a large enthusiastic cheering section of classmates, parents, family members and friends who had made the trip from Greenville. A smaller but equally vocal contingent of Edmunds fans had traveled 140 miles from Sumter to cheer on their team. The brick walls of Dobson Gymnasium reverberated with the screams of fans as the two teams entered the court.

As the Generals went through their pregame warm-ups, the Wade Hampton cheerleaders led the Generals' fans in a familiar musical chant:

Hoorah for Generals, Hoorah for Generals
Someone in the crowd is yelling Hoorah for Generals
One, two, three, four—who ya gonna yell for?
Generals, that's who!

The game started with both teams fighting championship game jitters. Edmunds led 10-9 at the end of the first quarter and then expanded that lead to 17-12. Coach Ross called a timeout to calm his team. He impressed upon them to relax and play their game. Ross reminded his team to force a faster tempo to the game to capitalize on Wade Hampton's superior depth.

Coming out of the timeout, Mayes rattled off six straight points, two of them on tip-ins when he reached high above the rim to follow up on missed shots. The Generals went on a 10-5 run after the timeout that allowed them to stake a 22-19 halftime lead. Ross spoke confidently to his team in the locker room, instructing them to continue the pace they had set in the final few minutes of the first half. Players and coaches could sense a state championship within their grasp.

As they had in the two previous state tournament games, the Generals came out hot in the early stages of the second half. Anderson scored five of his 13 points in the third quarter to put the Generals ahead 35-24 with a quarter to play. Midway through the third quarter, Mayes picked up his third personal foul, and Ross had to bench him.

"When Clyde got that third foul, I recall thinking about how well we had meshed with him as a team, but I wondered whether we could play well without him," MacDonald said.

MacDonald's fears were quickly put to rest as the Generals extended their lead to as many as 17 points in the final quarter. With the game comfortably in hand, Ross substituted freely. Edmunds was forced to foul late in the game, and the Generals sank 22 of 26 free-throw attempts to help secure the win.

Wade Hampton's defense held high-scoring guards Motley and Heriot to a combined six points, while their center, Kilby, scored only 10 points. Wade Hampton defeated Edmunds 60-46, earning the school's first state championship in any sport. Mayes finished with 20 points and 20 rebounds, and his sidekick Anderson had 13 points and 12 rebounds.

Perhaps the unsung hero of the tournament and even the season was junior point guard Spink. Standing only 5'8", Spink was the quarterback of the Generals' offense and typically drew a tough defensive assignment. He said, "I was never a great outside shooter but always was decent from the foul line." In the three state tournament games, Spink sank 19 of 21 free throws.

The role of the point guard on a basketball team is critical in establishing the tempo of the game and providing leadership on the court. Spink was an adept ball handler with an excellent feel for the flow of the game. During timeouts, Ross would often ask Spink for advice. While Wade Hampton had depth at other positions, Spink as their point guard was indispensable.

As time expired in the championship game, Wade Hampton fans

spilled onto the court to congratulate their state championship team. A core group of students that attended every game that season celebrated with their classmates. Cheerleaders hugged everyone in their path.

Coach Ross was lifted onto the shoulders of his players and handed a pair of scissors from the trainer's medical bag. With a single snip, he cut the first cord of the net hanging from the Generals' second-half basket. Then, one by one, each player was given the opportunity to cut a strand of the net before it fell from the rim.

The on-court celebration was interrupted by a formal trophy presentation. Ross had his two senior captains, Wing and Goodman, receive the championship trophy on behalf of the team. The players draped the net over the trophy and held it high in the air as their fans provided one final loud cheer of the night. Mayes was named the tournament MVP, and he joined teammate MacDonald on the all-tournament team.

Senior cheerleader Rita McKinney remembered staring across the court as the Wade Hampton players accepted the championship trophy.

"We had never really won anything at Wade Hampton. We were a fairly young school and had no great success in sports prior to that night. As I looked at that team, I just remember not seeing black or white, but seeing our team—a unified team that had finally brought Wade Hampton a championship."

The victory celebration continued on the bus ride home with players laughing and singing together, hoping the thrill of the championship evening would never end. The large state championship trophy, which featured a silver cup perched atop a wooden base, was passed around the bus, giving each player a chance to hold it and savor his moment in history. Shortly after midnight, Coach Carlisle steered the bus into the "jock lot" where a handful of their most loyal fans welcomed the champions home.

Wade Hampton outscored its three state tournament opponents 214-140. On Sunday, after winning the title, Ross discussed the state championship victory with Bob Ungericht of the *Greenville Piedmont*.

"Edmunds was a good basketball team," Ross told Ungericht, "but our board play and our defense was just too much for them. I felt our defense was outstanding all the way. When you give up only 46, 46 and 48 points in three games, you have to be playing pretty good defensive basketball. We worked hard on defense all year, and it paid off."

As Ross looked ahead, he could hope for a chance at a second title. "You know Wing and Goodman are the only two we lose who have played a lot, and I'm already looking forward to next season," Ross said.

Ross was selected as the state 4A basketball coach of the year, and Mayes earned the state 4A player of the year designation, despite playing in only nine games for the Generals. After receiving the award, Mayes was quoted in *The Hampton Herald*, Wade Hampton's student newspaper: "I am just happy that I was able to contribute to a good team. No one person made the team. I hope everybody understands that. The team I was on before was great and might have gone all the way, so I am glad to switch right over to a championship team."

Mayes then made a bold prediction: "I think next year we're going to be so tough that nobody will be able to touch us."

Mayes, Anderson, Allen, Mitchell and Starks had been Wade

160

Hampton students for only 18 days, and yet, in that short amount of time, they became a part of history. They were Wade Hampton's first black athletes and members of the school's first state championship team.

Anderson, Allen, Mitchell and Starks, along with Wing, Goodman, Barry Foy and Mel Tate, ended their high school basketball careers that evening in Spartanburg with a cherished championship memory. Juniors Mayes, MacDonald, Spink, Estes, Myers, McNamara and Ayers formed the nucleus of returning players that led Coach Ross to believe he had an outstanding chance to win back-to-back state championships.

———————

While Wade Hampton was capturing the 4A championship, Coach Ronnie Moore's J.L. Mann team won the boys 3A championship by defeating Summerville in a game played at Carolina Coliseum. It was the first of three state championships Moore won during his 21-year career as the head basketball coach at J.L. Mann.

When school resumed at these two Greenville schools the following Monday, students and faculty celebrated the success of these two integrated championship teams. The success of these two teams provided tangible examples of unity and cooperation between whites and blacks that occurred in Greenville shortly after the federal court's mandate to integrate the public schools.

Meanwhile, during the same week of the state basketball championships, violence and fear ripped through Lamar, South Carolina, a small rural town in Darlington County located about 160 miles from Greenville. Like Greenville County, Darlington County was ordered in January of 1970 by the federal government to integrate its school system in the middle of its school year. Schools in Lamar consisted of a white elementary and high school and a black elementary and high school. The integration plan forced the immediate transfer of all of the city's black students to the white schools.

On the morning of March 3, 1970, a mob of 150-200 white men and women wielding ax handles, chains, billy clubs and bricks gathered outside Lamar High School. They represented an organization that referred to itself as the "Darlington County Freedom-of-Choice Committee." As a bus carrying four black students pulled up to the school, members of the mob pelted it with bricks. A second bus with nearly 20 black students arrived a few minutes later, and members of the mob jumped on the hood and ripped off the bus's distributor cap. Other protesters began to shatter the windows of the bus with their ax handles. A third bus carrying another 15 black students arrived and was attacked in a similar manner by the mob. Law enforcement officials scuffled with the rioters as they attempted to rescue the children off the bus.

As the fighting intensified, blue-helmeted state highway patrolmen dispensed tear gas to drive away the rioters. Once the gas cleared, the patrolmen escorted the children inside the school as members of the mob shouted racial epithets. The mob regrouped and charged two of the empty buses, turning them both over. Highway patrolmen once again fired tear gas into the crowd, which caused them to disperse. A number of demonstrators and police received minor injuries in the scuffle, and a handful of students received cuts from shattered glass.

Forty male rioters were charged in the incident, but only three spent time in jail. The day after the violence broke out, the National Guard was placed at the school. The Lamar riots were considered one of the nation's most violent responses to the court-imposed de-segregation of public schools.

9
Interlude

If there is no struggle, there is no progress.

Frederick Douglass

Norman MacDonald and Clyde Mayes stretched their bodies out in the freshly mowed Bermuda grass in the track infield behind Wade Hampton High. It was a warm spring afternoon in 1970, and other than a mist of pollen blowing in the wind, the weather was close to perfect for an outdoor sporting event.

Track meets were lengthy affairs that provided participants large chunks of time to sit around while they waited for their next events. Mayes and MacDonald took these opportunities to get to know each other better. MacDonald told Mayes of his family's immigration from Scotland, and Mayes shared his story about growing up in Nicholtown. They talked about music, sports, plans for the summer and—of course—girls. Their friendship grew.

Spring sports were in full swing by late March, and nearly all of the Generals basketball players were participating. Mayes threw the shot put for Coach Johnny Ross's track team, and MacDonald competed in several running and jumping events. Billy Spink, Bobby Estes, Paul Myers and Johnny Ayers played for Coach Bill Phillips' baseball team. Tom Goodman was the captain of the tennis team, and George Poe was a member of the golf team.

As the school year came to a close, seniors made plans for life beyond high school. During this era, the dark reality of the ongoing conflict between the North and South Vietnamese hung over every American teenage male. It had been five years since the first U.S. Marines landed in Vietnam, and an end to the war was nowhere in sight.

On the evening of November 25, 1969, CBS News interrupted the network's regularly scheduled broadcast of "Mayberry RFD" to connect with a live feed from Washington reporter Roger Mudd who announced, "Good evening…Tonight, for the first time in 27 years, the United States has again started a draft lottery."

Similar lotteries were conducted until 1973 and led to more than two million men between the ages of 18 and 26 being selected for military service during the Vietnam War. As long as the conflict in Vietnam raged on, every young male in the country realized that any plans he made might be interrupted by an abrupt call to serve.

The draft fueled anti-war sentiments across America. Many draftees burned their draft cards or draft letters while others fled the country in order to avoid military service. Violent anti-war protests were commonplace, particularly on college campuses.

One of the most tragic anti-war riots occurred at Kent State University during the first four days of May 1970. On day four of the demonstration, members of the Ohio National Guard opened fire on protesters, killing four and wounding nine others. Two of the fatally wounded students had not actually participated in the protest. As a result of the Kent State tragedy, many college campuses cancelled classes for the remainder of the school year. President Richard Nixon said after the Kent State riots, "This should remind all once again that when dissent turns to violence, it invites tragedy."

Days after the tragedy at Kent State, the Wade Hampton community was grieving the sudden death of William Spink Sr., the patriarch of one of its most well-known families. On an unseasonably hot day in May of 1970, Spink suffered a fatal heart attack. He was 42. Billy Spink, who was 16 at the time, rode in the ambulance to the hospital with his mother as paramedics made an unsuccessful attempt to save his father's life. It was the second time in two years that a member of the basketball team had lost his father.

William Spink Sr. was born in Philadelphia in 1928, and both he and his wife Nancy were graduates of Ivy League schools: William from Princeton; Nancy, the University of Pennsylvania. William was an accomplished high school football and baseball player in the Philadelphia area. The Spink family, which included three sons and a daughter, moved to Greenville in 1963 when William accepted a job transfer from his employer, Monsanto. They bought a two-story, four-bedroom home on Vicki Circle in the same neighborhood as Billy's teammates, Paul Myers and Norman MacDonald.

Spink's sons, Peter, Billy and Bruce, were born two years apart, and remarkably, all share the same August 3rd birthday. All three played football, basketball and baseball for Wade Hampton, and from 1967 to 1973, at least one of the Spink boys was making a significant contribution on the football field, the basketball court or the baseball diamond for the Generals.

The Spinks were all of point guard stature, standing well short of six feet. They were not blessed with blinding speed or freakish athletic gifts, yet they possessed the intangibles that make an athlete a winner. Those qualities endeared them to their coaches and teammates. They were intelligent, intuitive and scrappy—born leaders who demonstrated poise and decisiveness in the heat of competition. Billy credits his father for instilling these skills and values in them.

"Our father coached us through our early years, and he imparted insights to us and taught us to be students of the game," Billy Spink said. "He would be our loudest cheerleader and our strongest critic because he wanted us to excel as he had done in the prep school system of Philadelphia. He drove me and my brothers to be the best that we could be, even if we weren't the most talented in the group."

Billy began his senior year of high school without his father and biggest fan— and without his lifelong mentor. Fortunately, the time and energy the elder Spink had invested in his sons' personal and athletic development continued to drive and guide them. While William's spirit lived on through his family, his absence at games, booster club events and impromptu sports activities in the neighborhood was conspicuous.

Point guard Billy Spink (23) launches a jump shot in a game at J.L. Mann during the 1969-70 season. (*Photo courtesy of the* Trevilian, *1970 Wade Hampton High School yearbook*)

Wade Hampton held graduation ceremonies for its Class of 1970 at Greenville Memorial Auditorium on May 28, recognizing its 714 graduates. At the time, it was the largest single class to graduate from a high school in the state of South Carolina. A separate valedictorian award was established for the black students who had transferred in from Washington High School.

The 1970 *Trevilian* commemorated the 10th anniversary of the school. While much of the planning for the yearbook was completed prior to desegregation, a two-page spread in the opening section highlighted the integration of the school and featured photos of the assembly that welcomed the new students in February.

Corrine Morrow Wiley served as the editor of the *Trevilian* and recalled the predicament facing her staff with the midyear addition of the new students.

"I remember Betty Workman, our journalism advisor, taking me and the editor of the school paper to Washington High to meet with the leaders of their publications," Wiley said. "When we got to Washington, we learned that they wanted to be included in the 'Trevilian.' However, the problem was that our cover was already made for 320 pages."

Wiley explained that it was cost prohibitive to resize the yearbook, and a decision was made that a separate yearbook for Washington High would be produced and sold to its former students who were then attending Wade Hampton.

Basketball recruiting letters for Clyde Mayes began to fill the mailbox at Wade Hampton's athletic offices. His performance in the state tournament drew the attention of major college programs across the country. Over the summer, he was invited to attend several summer basketball camps held on college campuses in the Carolinas. These camps not only gave Mayes a chance to improve his skills, but also allowed college coaches the opportunity to get a closer look at the gifted big man.

In mid-June, Mayes attended Coach Dick Campbell's Citadel basketball camp in Charleston. Campbell was in his second year at The Citadel after successful stints at North Greenville Junior College and Carson-Newman College in Tennessee. Included on Campbell's staff was Les Robinson, who would eventually succeed Campbell at The Citadel before serving as the head coach at East Tennessee State and NC State.

The Citadel camp had an excellent reputation for providing a sound instructional experience as well as meaningful competition for some of the best high school players in the state. Campers were housed in the Law Barracks, one of the original cadet housing facilities at The Citadel. It was named in honor of Evander M. Law, an 1856 graduate of The Citadel who served as a major general in the Confederate Army. The barracks consisted of four floors of rooms that opened to an outdoor walkway referred to by the cadets as a "galley." A large quadrangle of red and white checkerboard squares covered the ground floor in the center of the barracks.

Mayes' roommate at The Citadel camp was his archrival from Greenville High, Clyde Agnew. The two tall basketball players were crammed for the week into a narrow room that contained Spartan metal furniture, including standard-sized bunk beds. The rooms were not air-conditioned. A single window and a screen door provided the hope of a much-needed cross breeze during the humid summer nights.

Campers ranging in age from 10 to 18 arrived on Sunday afternoon, and Monday morning, they began a weeklong schedule of 12-hour days executing drills, competing in games and listening to instruction from coaches. Six baskets were set up on three courts in McAlister Fieldhouse. In the mornings, after a series of instructions and drills and a shooting competition, teams competed in half-court three-on-three games. Afternoons consisted of more instruction and drills and an occasional lecture or film. Evenings were for competitive five-on-five games.

Midway through the camp, Mayes' three-on-three team squared off against Agnew's team. The game occurred shortly before the lunch break, and many of the other campers had already completed their morning activities. As the game neared its end, all of the remaining campers and coaches had encircled the court and were watching intently as the camp's two biggest stars fought to earn bragging rights in the three-on-three competition.

The rules of the game were simple. Each basket counts a point, and the first team to 21 wins—but you must win by two baskets. Possession was governed by what players called "make it take it," which meant so long as you scored, you kept possession of the ball. After the rebound of a missed shot by the non-shooting team, the ball had to be cleared past the foul line before a shot could be attempted. Officiating was governed by the honor system with players calling their own fouls. One team wore T-shirts, and the other did not, forming the familiar playground monikers of "shirts and skins."

Agnew's strategy against Mayes was to draw him from the basket to neutralize the strength of his rival's inside game. Agnew possessed an excellent shot, which forced Mayes to extend his defense to the perimeter. Mayes relied on his muscle to back Agnew down low under the basket where he would either use a simple drop-step move to score a layup or shoot a soft short-range bank shot over Agnew.

With Agnew's team up by a point, Mayes missed a short jump shot, and Agnew grabbed the rebound. He tossed it to a teammate at the foul line who then fired it back to Agnew who had drifted to the corner. Agnew caught the pass and squared his shoulders as he leapt into the air. Mayes rushed toward him, jumping up with both arms extended. Agnew pulled the ball well behind his head and leaned away from the oncoming Mayes. The ball floated off Agnew's fingertips, just outside Mayes' outstretched hands. The crowd of campers and coaches stared at the ball as it arched its way toward the basket. Agnew's shot was perfect.

The campers surrounding the court erupted with applause and cheers for what was clearly the most intense competition of the week between the camp's two best players. It would be a rare victory for Agnew in the ongoing "Battle of the Clydes."

In the Deep South, football has always been the most popular sport. It draws more media attention and hype than all other sports combined. More budget dollars in high schools and colleges are directed to the football program than any other sport. Fathers in the South dream of their sons becoming football heroes.

The landscape of South Carolina is dotted with small towns whose communities unify around their high school football teams. Barbershops and "meat-and-three" restaurants are filled daily with old-timers who enjoy the weekly retelling of their glory days of playing high school football. In Upstate towns like Woodruff, Easley and Greer, businesses were known to shut down early on Fridays in preparation for evening football games. The rivalry between Greenville's two oldest high schools, Greenville and Parker, featured an annual football match-up that from 1947 to 1967 was held on Thanksgiving Day at Greenville's Sirrine Stadium. The game, known as the "Turkey Bowl," routinely attracted an overflow crowd in excess of 15,000 people.

Wade Hampton's football history was unremarkable. Prior to 1970, the Generals had compiled a 10-year overall record of 32-64-8 and had posted only three winning seasons. In 1968, however, the Generals led by future University of Georgia running back Robert Honeycutt, had their best season to date, finishing 8-2. The following year, under new head coach Bill Phillips, the Generals finished 6-3-1, giving them their first back-to-back winning seasons. Desegregation brought a new crop of competitors, and capturing a state basketball championship in 1970 ignited a winning attitude among the school's athletes. Optimism ran high as two-a-day football practices began in the August heat.

Clyde Mayes played football at Beck, but none of the Wade Hampton coaches had seen him play in person. They were unsure if he had the skills to play for Wade Hampton, so Clyde was asked to take part in an impromptu tryout before the end of his junior year. Mayes joined a couple of returning football players at the school's stadium, and he was put through a series of basic agility and catching drills. Assistant Football Coach John Carlisle oversaw the workout.

"I remember they couldn't find any cleats that would fit me, so I had to work out in a pair of sneakers," Mayes recalled. "It made me mad at first that they put me through that tryout, and I didn't really want to play football, but they talked me into it."

It didn't take long for Carlisle to realize Mayes' athleticism, coupled with his size, would make him an asset to the football team. Carlisle smiled throughout the workout as he pondered Mayes roaming the defensive secondary snagging or deflecting the other team's passes. Offensively, Mayes would provide a can't-miss target for the Generals' passing attack. The most difficult task facing Coach Carlisle and Coach Phillips was telling Coach Ross his star basketball player was planning to play football. Wade Hampton football games were going to be difficult for Coach Ross to watch as Mayes joined six other basketball players on the Generals' football squad.

Johnny Ayers from the basketball team was the starting quarterback. MacDonald and Spink played in both the offensive and defensive backfield. Mayes (6'7") and Will McNamara (6'4") played end, giving the Generals the tallest pair of receivers in the conference. Mayes also played safety on defense and was positioned just below the crossbar of the goal post when opposing teams attempted a field goal so he could use his size and leaping ability to swat away anything within his reach.

In the Generals' third game of the season against Hillcrest, Spink took part in a play that he remembered as his favorite of the season. It involved a combination of three players who had joined forces to bring Wade Hampton the state basketball championship the previous March. Early in the first quarter, Coach Phillips called for a halfback option. Quarterback Johnny Ayers made a quick pitch to halfback MacDonald. As MacDonald rolled out, he spotted Spink open in the flat and fired a perfect spiral. Spink collected the pass and raced upfield. Around the Hillcrest 28-yard line, he was hemmed in by a group of defenders. Before being tackled, Spink tossed the ball backward to Mayes, who collected it in stride and raced into the end zone.

Teammates Billy Spink (21), Clyde Mayes (85) and Norman MacDonald (42) are shown taking a break during a football practice during the 1970 season. *(Photo courtesy of Norman MacDonald)*

The Generals began their 1970 football season with nine straight victories, defeating their opponents by a combined score of 300-28. Seven of their first nine wins were shutouts. After defeating Parker High 27-0, legendary Parker Coach White Kendall said, "I would say Wade Hampton is the best area prep team in a decade." Midway through the season, Head Coach Bill Phillips, in an interview with columnist Dan Foster of *The Greenville News*, praised his talented team. "The unity of this team is outstanding, and the one big thing is they love to play," Phillips said.

After its 9-0 start, Wade Hampton rose to number two in both state wire service polls, setting up the season's most critical match-up against T.L. Hanna. The winner of the game would advance to the state playoffs as the Region II champion.

On a warm soggy night at Wade Hampton Stadium, an overflow crowd in excess of 11,000 witnessed the Generals and Yellow Jackets lock up in a defensive struggle. The lone score in the game was a 31-yard field goal by T.L. Hanna tackle Buck Thompson with 3:40 left to play in the game. It was the first and only time all season that Wade Hampton had fallen behind in a game. Earlier in the contest, Wade Hampton missed an attempt at a 31-yard field goal.

Wade Hampton had two final attempts to score, but both drives were thwarted by interceptions. Jim Ed Rice, a 6'2" 175-pound defensive back, recorded one of Hanna's late-game interceptions. Rice transferred to Hanna from Westside High at the start of the school year when Anderson County schools were integrated. The following June, after graduating from Hanna, Rice was picked in the first round of baseball's free-agent draft by the Boston Red Sox. He played 16 seasons for the Red Sox and was named to the all-star team eight times. Rice was selected as the 1978 American League MVP. In 2009, the Anderson native was inducted into the Major League Baseball Hall of Fame.

While both teams finished the season with 10-1 overall records and 7-1 conference records, Hanna received the conference crown as a result of its head-to-head victory over Wade Hampton. The loss to Hanna ended the Generals' dream of advancing to the state championship and earning the rare distinction of holding the state football and basketball crowns at the same time. T.L. Hanna was defeated by

Eau Claire in the Upper State Championship.

During the week following the game, Wade Hampton officials became aware of information questioning the eligibility of some of Hanna's players. Coach Phillips filed an official protest with the State High School League, but the issue was ruled an "administrative oversight," dashing any final hopes for Wade Hampton to keep its season alive.

Fifty years after the game, the loss remains a painful memory in Wade Hampton's sports history. The sting was worsened for Norman MacDonald during a chance encounter with Vincent Price, who was the head linesman on the officiating crew that night.

"I ran into Price in a business meeting many years after that game," MacDonald recalled. "He remembered me from that game, and he said he needed to apologize for something that happened that night."

Price, who was also a highly regarded college football official, told MacDonald about a mistake that continued to haunt him. On the play before Hanna kicked its winning field goal, a Yellow Jacket back ran a sweep toward the Wade Hampton sideline. The ball carrier ran out of bounds near the 14-yard line. When Price spotted the ball for the fourth down field-goal attempt, he placed it in the center of the hash marks instead of on the right hash mark, thus allowing Hanna's Thompson a straight-on kick as opposed to a more difficult kick from the right hash. The field was muddy after a week of intermittent rain, and it was the first field goal Thompson had attempted all year.

At the end of the season, MacDonald was selected to the Region II 4A first team offense and earned honorable mention on defense. Spink, Mayes, Ayers and McNamara, along with seven of their Generals teammates, earned honorable mention on the all-region team with Spink and Mayes being recognized on both offense and defense.

MacDonald was also picked to play in the prestigious Shrine Bowl, which pitted the best high school players in South Carolina against their counterparts in North Carolina. Mayes' size and athleticism drew the attention of Division I football coaches, who directed a steady stream of letters to the school's athletic offices in an effort to entice Mayes into playing college football instead of college basketball.

The Generals ended their football season the week after the Hanna game with a 34-0 win over the Southside Tigers. Prior to the game, the Wade Hampton cheerleaders stretched out a colorful banner under the goal post that read: "Thanks Generals, For the Best Year Yet."

During the week leading up to the Wade Hampton-T.L. Hanna football game, Greenville County's first-year school superintendent, J. Floyd Hall, was in the midst of one of the most stressful times of his life. The 45-year-old Hall accepted the superintendent's position in Greenville after M.T. Anderson stepped down as a result of health-related issues at the end of the 1969-70 school year.

Hall was born in 1925 in Langdale, Alabama. His father worked in a textile mill and supported his family on $12 a week. Hall remembers attending his first day of school barefoot and wearing his only pair of bib overalls. For most of his childhood, the Halls' rural home did not have the comfort of an indoor bathroom.

Following high school, Hall served in the U.S. Air Force from 1943 to 1945, and thanks to the G.I. Bill, he was able to attend college at Alabama Polytechnical Institute, later renamed Auburn University. He began his career in education as a high school teacher and coach in Lanett, Alabama. In over five decades as an educator and administrator, it was the only position for which Hall would have to apply. He moved from Lanett in 1951 when he accepted his first position in school administration as an assistant principal in the Fairfax (Alabama) School System. In 1958, he moved his family to Puerto Rico where he became the superintendent of schools at the Ramey Air Force Base. In his memoir, *In My Wildest Dreams, The Life Story of J. Floyd Hall, Ed.D.,* he explained his early experiences working in the segregated South and his move to Puerto Rico.

> *Discrimination was evident in the school system in Fairfax as it was elsewhere. ...Living through that period of history where people were not respected and treated equally played a major role in my decision to accept the position as superintendent of schools at Ramey Air Force Base.*

In 1960, Hall left Puerto Rico to become the assistant school superintendent in Evanston, Illinois. He was paid $12,500 with a promise that his salary would double within five years; his salary doubled within two years.

Hall built a solid reputation as an effective school administrator, and, in 1967, the nearby Oak Park-River Forest High School District lured him away to become their superintendent. In early 1970, a search committee from the Greenville County School District reached out to Hall to see if he would be interested in the superintendent's position in Greenville. Hall declined, stating emphatically that he had no interest in leaving the Chicago area.

The Greenville delegation was persistent, certain that Hall was their man for the job. A member of the search committee showed up unannounced at Hall's Oak Park office and convinced him to at least make an exploratory visit to Greenville. Local Greenville advertising executive Jim Henderson prepared a film especially for Hall, highlighting all of the attractive aspects of the Greenville community. Hall consented to a visit, but he told the delegate from Greenville that he had absolutely no interest in making a move. Hall made a second visit to Greenville, and after what he said involved, "much discussion, deep consideration and sincere prayer," he agreed to accept the position.

Hall explained his decision to come to Greenville in his memoir: "I had left Alabama because of my opposition to the way black children and blacks, in general, were treated. I chose to work in integrated schools, including Evanston. One of the reasons I came to Greenville was the court order requiring integration. I knew it was to be an integrated school system, and I wanted to help make that happen."

Hall and his wife Margaret had two sons. Their first son, Mike, was attending the University of Kansas when the family moved to Greenville, and Reggie was entering the sixth grade. Reggie's first school assignment in Greenville was at Nicholtown Elementary, which was serving as one of a handful of sixth-grade centers after integration. Hall acknowledged that the move was a difficult one for his son but praised the efforts and kindness of his sixth-grade teacher at Nicholtown, Gloria Banks, for easing his son's transition. The Halls began to construct a new home on Greenville's East Side in the Foxcroft subdivision.

Mike described his father as a "born crusader" whose strong Christian faith drove him to do the right thing even when faced with significant opposition.

"As a young boy, I remember he would drive me out to some rural areas of Alabama and show me the difficult living conditions of many of the black residents," Hall said. "He told me, 'This has to change. We have to do something about this.' The fact that the Greenville County schools were in the midst of integration was an attractive challenge for him to undertake."

Hall admitted that he did not have a full appreciation for the underlying tension that remained in the Greenville community post integration.

> *I did not realize all the hard work that was to come during that first year because I was led to believe that most of the shock of integration had worn off—that there were some minor differences, but nothing as radical as we faced. Things would have been smoother had some agitators from other areas not become involved.*

Hall's first board meeting at the school district gave him an indication of the lingering racial tension in Greenville County schools. He describes it in detail in his memoir.

> *There were two men (who were not board members) sitting and listening to the business transactions that day. One raised his hand, approached the board and said he had something to present. It turned out to be a petition… The petition basically stated: We demand the board send Floyd Hall and all of his nigger friends back to D.C. That was my welcome to Greenville. That individual later ran for the school board and was elected.*

Parker and Berea High Schools were located in communities that served primarily longtime or lifelong white residents of Greenville. Prior to integration, Parker High's enrollment of 1,193 included only 17 black students, while Berea had only 11 black students among a population of 1,185. Integration had been deferred until the fall of 1970 for both of these schools.

As the 1970-71 school year began, and whites and blacks mixed for the first time on these campuses, groups of angry white citizens began to organize and issue demands upon the school district. Included in the list of demands presented to Hall was that "Dixie," the theme song of the Confederacy, continue to be played at high school football games.

Also, reports began to surface that many blacks were unhappy about the inequities resulting from the integration plan. Reportedly, civil rights advocates from outside Greenville began to meet locally throughout the black community of Greenville, planting seeds for concern. When Hall arrived in Greenville, he was sympathetic to the plight of the black students and began to immediately set up bi-racial committees in each school. Hall assessed in his autobiography the underlying sentiments present in the schools.

> *Imagine a previously all-black school, with the head cheerleader, star athlete or anyone holding a student office, suddenly thrown into a school that had been predominately white. The students who were already in that particular school had held most of those positions. ...Some had to give up the school they had attended all their lives. Others were moved out of a community and the young black children took the brunt of busing. Some were bused*

long distances in outlying school districts.

In early November of 1970, the pent-up anger and tension over school integration in Greenville County had reached its boiling point. A school integration process that was described in the national media as one of "grace and style" was about to give way to violence and chaos.

10
November 1970

This is the first time I've ever had to have armed guards at schools—but it's the only way we could keep the schools open.

Dr. J. Floyd Hall

November 1970

The Atkins family lived in a quiet cul-de-sac in a one-story brick home on Prince Charming Drive, a block from the main entrance to Berea Junior and Senior High. John Atkins was a 16-year-old junior at Berea, and his two younger sisters, Pam and Cindy, were in the fifth and fourth grade, respectively at nearby Berea Elementary.

The Atkins' neighborhood consisted of two parallel streets that ended in cul-de-sacs, Prince Charming Drive and Enchanted Circle. They were connected by a cross street, Cinderella Lane. A school bus dropped Pam and Cindy off near their home each weekday afternoon around 3 o'clock. While they waited for their parents and brother to arrive home, the two young girls occupied their time by playing in their backyard with Duke, their faithful German Shepherd, or roaming the neighborhood with a group of friends. It was a safe neighborhood where people never locked their doors, and neighbors looked out for one another. On a warm clear Friday in November of 1970, the Atkins' idyllic existence in a neighborhood with street names inspired by fairy tales was rudely interrupted.

As Pam and Cindy walked through the door of their home, the

phone was ringing. Their mother was calling from work. She frantically instructed her two young daughters to immediately go through the house, lock all the doors and windows and pull the curtains. She told her children that under no conditions were they to leave the house and that she was leaving work to be with them. When asked why she was giving these panicked instructions, she said simply, "There's been a riot at the high school."

"It was a scary moment. We had no idea what was going on just up the street, so we did what our mother told us," Pam Atkins Harrison recalled. "My sister and I peeked out from behind the curtains at our front window trying to see what was happening. Our brother hadn't gotten home, and we worried if he was caught up in the riot."

Berea High is about six miles west of Downtown Greenville. Approximately 1,500 students, including 321 blacks, attended grades 7-12 at Berea in the fall of 1970. The majority of the black high school students came to Berea from the former Sterling High in Downtown Greenville. From the day the new black students set foot on the Berea campus, tensions ran high. Disputes and fights between whites and blacks were everyday occurrences. In September and October, there were approximately 165 student suspensions at Berea.

Blacks were upset about the playing of "Dixie" at school events and their lack of representation in student organizations. There were reports of black students bullying smaller white students, and a group of white cheerleaders claimed that some of their black classmates had threatened to cut off their hair. Similar reports of white students harassing and bullying black students were also commonplace within the school during this time.

A group of white parents calling themselves the "Concerned Parents Association" began holding meetings to discuss problems at

Berea. On Sunday, October 25, 175 people met on the campus to discuss what they termed "a lack of protection for students within the school." A second meeting was held the following Sunday afternoon with about 150 gathering at the home of Henry W. Bayne at 311 Rainbow Drive. The group obtained over 700 signatures on a petition that requested the establishment of an 11-person committee to represent the association in any cases involving student protection.

The school's homecoming football game was scheduled for Friday evening, November 6. Several black students claimed they were told by whites that if they attended the game, they would be attacked. Also, during the week leading up to homecoming, the concerned citizens group presented the school administration with a list of specific demands, including a request that the sheriff's office place full-time guards at the school. The group also requested that "Dixie" continue to be played at all football games.

A group of black parents held a meeting the night before homecoming at the Birnie Street YWCA. A leaflet was distributed, telling black parents, "White folk said they want more severe punishment for black students, and if the school won't do it, they will do it themselves." This prompted a group of black students to request a meeting with school officials.

The following morning, Berea Principal Homer Voyles met with several black students in an open courtyard. While the meeting was taking place, reports within the school began to circulate that students were becoming unruly, turning over trashcans and running through the halls. Voyles attempted to move the meeting into the school gymnasium to provide a controlled setting for discussions. Officers from the Greenville County Sheriff's Department arrived on the scene at approximately 9 a.m., but school officials requested they leave the campus so as not to incite any further unrest. The sheriff's deputies complied with the school's request only to be summoned back to campus 45 minutes later when further chaos and fighting occurred.

Members of the white parents' group heard about the meeting with Voyles and began to show up on campus. Many of them were carrying tire irons and pipes. One white parent was arrested for carrying a .22 caliber pistol on campus. Meanwhile, a fight between black and white students broke out in a classroom. A photo of this classroom appeared in the afternoon paper, the *Greenville Piedmont*, showing the room's disordered condition after the fight. As news of the classroom fight spread across campus, a number of other skirmishes between whites and blacks took place.

The early edition of the *Greenville Piedmont* pieced together a sketchy report on the events that transpired that morning at Berea. The following is an excerpt from their article that ran under the headline, "Whites with Clubs Reported at Berea."

> *Berea High School was closed at mid-morning today because of disturbances on campus.*
>
> *Early reports indicate that a group of white citizens arrived at the school early today armed with clubs and began breaking into classrooms to get the blacks.*
>
> *Dr. J. Floyd Hall, school superintendent, ordered the school closed today and postponed tonight's football game.*

In his memoir, Superintendent Hall recalled that day at Berea, saying that one member of the citizens' committee and one of his cronies, "broke out windows and pulled white students through the windows, telling them to get out, or awful things would happen to them."

As students were dismissed from class by 11 a.m., parents rushed to the school to pick up their children. By noon, the campus was deserted, and a line of sheriff's patrol cars surrounded the campus.

Superintendent Hall issued the following public comment:

> *I am greatly disturbed that a group of citizens has brought on this kind of disturbance for the last few weeks in the Berea High School community. The District plans to hold legally responsible these individuals who were responsible for this disturbance. We urge the support of all citizens of the Greenville Community in settling our differences and bringing about responsible action from all citizens of Greenville County.*

Berea's homecoming football game against Pickens High was rescheduled to Saturday afternoon at a neutral site, Wade Hampton High School. A contingent of highway patrolmen, sheriff's deputies and armed guards was on hand for the game but was not needed as the game and surrounding festivities were conducted without incident. Pickens defeated Berea 26-0.

Classes were again cancelled on Monday, November 9, but resumed the next day and operated on a shortened half-day schedule. A ring of law enforcement officers from the county and state surrounded the school that rainy morning, ensuring that only students were permitted to enter the grounds. The school reported an approximate absentee rate of 50 percent on Tuesday.

Principal Voyles said he believed that as long as the school was permitted to run without interference from parents, either black or white, it could maintain normal operations. Additional precautionary measures were taken when school resumed, including assigning a faculty member or adult volunteer to ride each school bus and placing security at the school around the clock. As the unrest at Berea began to settle, problems at neighboring high schools were just beginning.

J.L. Mann High School was located near the affluent Parkins Mill Road section of Greenville. It opened in 1965 and was named in honor of James Lewis Mann who served as the superintendent of Greenville County Schools from 1916 to 1940. In February of 1970, Mann's seventh and eighth-graders were transferred to Beck Junior High, and the majority of Beck's 10th-12th-grade students were reassigned to Mann, giving Mann an approximate 75-25 white to black student ratio. Jack Chandler was a 10th-grade student at Mann when school desegregation took place, and he remembered the school's first integrated pep rally.

"We gathered in the gym, and all the blacks sat on one side and the whites on the other. Our principal stood in the middle of the basketball court, trying to help us find some common ground. He suggested each group do a favorite cheer," Chandler said. "We whites went first and did a typical low volume, low energy cheer. Then, the Beck transfers did their cheer, and I'll never forget it. It raised the roof. The cheer went on for a couple of minutes and was very much like music, though they were cheering. Their voices rang like a bell and literally raised goosebumps on my arms. I heard various folks on our side say variations of: 'Well, we're not in Kansas anymore.'"

Chandler recalled that, in the first days of integration, there were some mild disturbances, but overall, school proceeded without interruption. Around midday on Tuesday, November 17, approximately 200 white and black students began chanting and running around in the school cafeteria. They were instructed to return to class, but many of them wandered outside the school grounds onto an adjacent street. Law enforcement officials were called to the scene and utilized tear gas to disperse the crowd of protesters. One black student was injured when he was hit in the head by a brick, and three arrests were made.

Earlier that same morning at Greenville High, approximately 100 black students were suspended for walking out of class and breaking windows. Their walkout reportedly was related to whether or not the word "Dixie" would remain in the school's alma mater. Four students were arrested as a result of the walkout, and over 100 were suspended. Later in the day, about 35 persons marched on the city jail in protest of the four arrests. Three of the marchers were arrested after police confiscated a .30 caliber carbine and two shotguns.

The mildest of the November 17 outbreaks occurred at Wade Hampton High School where approximately 50 students walked out of classes around 10 a.m. After talking to the students in the cafeteria, Principal Dewey Huggins said they all returned to class. These students requested a change in the school mascot and school colors, along with the initiation of a black culture program. There were no suspensions as a result of the protest.

In a related incident, a Wade Hampton bus driver was suspended for taking an unauthorized trip in a school bus. Also, a pair of 22-year-old white men armed with a shotgun were arrested after they attempted to board a school bus headed to Wade Hampton High. Earlier that morning, the same two men pointed a shotgun at a janitor at Paris Elementary and threatened him. Later that week, the two men were arrested and held without bond by the Greenville County sheriff.

The following morning at Parker High, a fight between whites and blacks broke out in a corridor near the principal's office where black students were presenting a list of demands to school officials. Their mandates included the discontinuance of the playing of "Dixie" at school events, a revised grading system and the establishment of a black culture program. School officials broke up the fight before the police arrived, and two white students were sent to the hospital with minor injuries. A series of other skirmishes occurred throughout the campus. A few minor cuts and bruises were reported, but no students involved were hospitalized.

Law enforcement officials dressed in riot gear attempt to control a crowd of protesting students on Bramlett Avenue near Parker High School on the morning of November 18, 1970.
(Photo courtesy of the Parkerscope, *1971 Parker High School yearbook)*

After the fights were broken up, approximately 200 students congregated outside the school. Fifty law enforcement officers were sent to Parker to help restore order. They arrived dressed in full riot gear including helmets, protective shields and billy clubs. Within a few minutes, they were able to disperse the crowd of students and restore order to the campus. An unidentified black man in an out-of-state vehicle was reported on school grounds and was suspected of being connected to the disturbances.

A series of minor isolated incidents was also reported at several other Greenville County schools on Wednesday, November 18. Two white men were arrested near Carolina High School after firing shots from a rifle aimed toward school security guards around 3 a.m. At Sevier Middle School, two juveniles were arrested for carrying knives, a blackjack and other weapons onto the school property. In Greer, two youths were arrested for calling in a bomb threat to a school. Minor fighting incidents were reported at Sans Souci Junior High. By Thursday, reports of protests and fighting had generally subsided throughout the school district.

While no conclusive evidence exists that connects each of these incidents, the timing of the outbreaks and the common themes of the demands that were raised at each school indicate a level of coordination and planning. A black student at one of the schools told *The Greenville News* that the protests had been planned through a series of meetings held at the Birnie Street YWCA. School Board Chairman T.G. Chappelear made the following public comment: "We feel the disruptions are partly due to a planned program by nonstudents in the county."

The media picked up quickly on the reports of Greenville's school protests, and wire stories appeared in newspapers across the nation.

Six months earlier, Greenville had been hailed nationally for the manner in which it peacefully handled school integration. The city's reputation for a near incident-free integration process was tarnished.

In the aftermath of these outbreaks, citizens of Greenville County took an anxious deep breath, not knowing if their community was on the verge of a season of race-related violence. Business leaders feared the incidents would jeopardize future economic investment.

The December 7, 1970 issue of *U.S. News and World Report* further shined the national spotlight on the Greenville situation. The cover featured a bold teaser in large blue and red letters that read: "All Desegregation Orders Obeyed—Then School Chaos in Greenville, S.C." On page 26, the story began with the following introduction in bold black letters:

> *It was called a model of integration in the South. But suddenly there were racial battles, walkouts, protests and police patrols. Here is a first-hand report of what went wrong.*

The article contained a series of quotes from white and black students at the county's high schools. Patricia Clark, a 17-year-old senior, described her experience as a black student at Wade Hampton:

"At Wade Hampton, everything is slavery time. Tension has been below the surface—then, it just broke out all at once. There's not been much fighting there, and I'll tell you why—because we're so outnumbered."

Greg Barksdale, a 17-year-old black senior at Greenville High, said, "Students are fed up with having to take what is handed out to them by the white man. We'd like black studies mandatory for all students."

Dewey Huggins, the principal at Wade Hampton, assessed the situation in the article. "We were making progress until we got some groups in town trying to polarize people. Black students came to me and told me when things would take place at all the high schools—the exact timetable. That means there is someone behind it," he said.

Superintendent Hall told a reporter from *U.S. News and World Report,* "I've never encountered these kinds of troubles in 23 years as an educator. This is the first time I've ever had to have armed guards at schools—but it's the only way we could keep the schools open."

No one was more determined to keep Greenville schools operational in the midst of the outbreaks than Superintendent Hall. The day after the protests, in *The Greenville News,* Hall stated his clear intent. "The education of our students is of paramount importance and shall be continued at all costs." Hall explained that steps had been taken to ensure adequate protection would be provided in all the schools. Despite Hall's assurances, absenteeism remained high at the affected schools for the remainder of the week. At Parker High, nearly 700 of its 1,250 students were absent on the day after the protests and fighting.

Hall appointed a pair of ombudsmen, one black and one white, to be his "eyes and ears" within the schools and to assist him with conciliatory efforts between the races. He directed efforts to bring black studies into the classroom and required that a biracial committee be established at each school.

Hall's support of integration in the Greenville County schools was steadfast, but it did not come without challenges and personal cost to Hall and his family. He called his first two years in Greenville "two of the hardest years I've ever spent in education."

"It was a very difficult time for my dad and our family," Hall's son Mike recalled. "I remember people putting 'For Sale' signs in our front yard and my mom not being able to really go out in public."

Ron Goodwin, a former teacher at Wade Hampton, worked alongside Dr. Hall as his director of transportation during the difficult years of school integration. "Dr. Hall was a natural leader who was always committed to doing the right thing," Goodwin said. "Sometimes that got him crossways with various people, but he always stuck to what he believed was right. He was really good for Greenville and a tremendous help to our community."

Following the November events, the same spirit of resilience and leadership that occurred during the previous February began to emerge. Led by Superintendent Hall, Greenville's community leaders quickly organized and committed to not stepping backward in their efforts to create a unified school system.

A broad-based group of citizens and government officials began meeting immediately to develop solutions to ease the racial tension in the schools. The day after the incidents, Mayor Cooper White held a meeting downtown that brought together a cross section of white and black community leaders to attempt to discuss the key issues that led to the protests. White expressed hope that meetings of that nature "bring them through—more than the National Guard or a show of force."

One of the prominent black leaders Mayor White called upon for help during this time was Theo Mitchell, who is a 1956 graduate of Sterling High School and a graduate of Fisk University and Howard Law School. After working for a time in Washington, D.C., Mitchell returned to Greenville in 1969 and opened a law practice. Earlier in 1970, he was elected president of the Greenville Urban League, an advocacy organization aimed at helping blacks and other underserved communities.

"We knew that violence was not the answer. We knew we had to find a peaceful answer to the challenges we were facing," Mitchell recalled. "Rational minds had to come together and deal with our problems. We had a slogan we came up with that said, 'We must work together, stand together and grow together.'"

Mitchell also praised Dr. Hall for his resilience during this era, calling him a "dynamic and courageous leader who stayed the course." Mitchell went on to serve in the South Carolina General Assembly from 1975 to 1995.

Officials from the South Carolina Law Enforcement Division, the National Guard and local authorities met to coordinate their response. Approximately 150 members of the 151st Signal Battalion of the National Guard arrived in Greenville and were placed on ready alert during the week of the protests. Armed law enforcement officials were assigned to each of the affected schools when they were reopened. By the weekend, calm set in over the Greenville schools, and there would be no more riots or outbursts of significance during the school year.

On the campus of Wade Hampton High School, responsibility for maintaining order fell heavily on the shoulders of 24-year-old Assistant Principal Brodie Bricker. He believed that "early intervention" and communication were the keys to averting potentially explosive situations. Bricker equipped his fellow assistant principals with walkie-talkies to utilize as they patrolled the school grounds. They used a series of Greek code words to help identify the nature of an emerging situation. Bricker said administrators and faculty were assigned to ride school buses that delivered students to the black neighborhoods during the period of unrest in the schools.

Bricker credited student leaders who provided needed inside information on potential threats. "Thankfully, we had some key student leaders, such as Clyde Mayes, who were committed to helping us keep order on the campus," Bricker said. "Clyde would tell me sometimes where and when I needed to be in order to stop something from happening."

In the midst of the November protests, Head Basketball Coach Johnny Ross was holding tryouts to select the members of his 1970-71 varsity basketball squad. Ross's team returned four starters from the previous year's state championship team, and he knew he had an excellent chance to win back-to-back titles. Excitement surrounding the basketball team provided a needed diversion from the unsettling events of a tumultuous week.

11
New Edition

Good teams become great ones when the members trust each other enough to surrender the me for the we.

Phil Jackson

Johnny Ross stood near midcourt at the bottom of a section of the wooden bleachers in the Wade Hampton gym in early November of 1970. He peered across several rows of boys wearing gym shorts, T-shirts and sneakers, all of them vying for a spot on Coach Ross's 1970-71 Wade Hampton Generals basketball team.

Ross held a clipboard bearing the names of all the hopefuls. Included among those trying out were four returning starters and three additional lettermen from last year's 4A state championship team. With a straight face, Ross told the boys nobody was guaranteed a spot on the team and that their efforts in the three days of tryouts would determine who would receive one of the 15 available uniforms. It was the kind of well-intended but barely believable statement most coaches delivered on the first day of tryouts, hoping to inspire a spirited effort by all.

Ross stood alongside Lynn Howard, his new assistant coach. Longtime assistant John Carlisle had accepted a position as the assistant director of transportation for the Greenville County School District, and in 1974, he became the head football coach and athletic director at Greenville's new Eastside High School, positions he held until his retirement in 2006.

Ross was 46 years old and beginning his 21st year of teaching and coaching. Howard was 27, and this was his first high school basketball coaching position. Ross was 5'6", balding with a physique beginning to display the normal effects of middle age. Howard was 6'3" with a full head of neatly combed dark hair and a lean athletic build, derived from years of playing competitive tennis. Ross was emotive at times. Players remember his face getting red with anger over a bad call or a player's repeated mistake. Howard was quiet and always in control of his emotions. Despite their differences, the two men quickly forged an effective coaching partnership and a deep personal friendship.

Ross and Howard, along with a second assistant, James Andrews, who joined them in 1972, led the Wade Hampton boys basketball program through the decade of the '70s and established it as one of the most successful high school programs in South Carolina. In Ross and Howard's first four years together, Wade Hampton's boys teams won 92 games while losing only 12, as they reeled off four consecutive 20-win seasons. In their 10 years sitting beside each other on the bench, Ross and Howard were 289-72, winning one state title in 1971, finishing second in 1974 and capturing five conference championships.

Howard was a native of Maryville, Tennessee, a town located about 20 miles south of the campus of the University of Tennessee in Knoxville. He developed a lifelong allegiance to the Volunteer sports teams and attended their football and basketball games regularly as a youth. Howard excelled as a tennis player at Maryville College, and his accomplishments on the tennis court from 1962 to 1966 led to his induction into its Athletic Hall of Fame in 1998.

Howard obtained his degree in mathematics and began his high school teaching and coaching career in 1966 at Ribault High School in north Jacksonville, Florida. After one year at Ribault where he taught math and coached tennis, he spent two years fulfilling the same responsibilities two hours south of Jacksonville at Titusville High School. At both Titusville and Ribault, Howard was present for racial integration.

Howard relocated to Greenville in 1969, taking a job as a math teacher at Wade Hampton while also beginning the pursuit of his master's degree at Furman University. In his second year at Wade Hampton, he joined Ross on the basketball staff as the head junior varsity coach and assistant varsity coach. Howard also began coaching tennis in his second year at Wade Hampton and coached the boys and girls tennis teams off and on for the next 26 years. In 1978, he took over as the head coach of the girls basketball team and served in that role for 10 of the next 17 years. In 1986, Howard succeeded Bill Phillips as the athletic director at Wade Hampton, a position he held until his retirement in 1996. Howard taught accelerated math classes including advanced algebra and trigonometry and, in time, became the school's advanced placement calculus teacher.

Howard was a student of the game of basketball and recalled watching Tennessee basketball and making mental notes on the offensive and defensive schemes employed by legendary coach Ray Mears. The Volunteers under Mears ran multiple versions of a trapping 1-3-1 defense. Howard implemented Mears' defensive philosophy on nearly every team he coached at Wade Hampton.

"Johnny was more of the motivator, and I was the strategy guy," Howard said of their coaching partnership. "We got along very well and complemented each other as coaches."

At practice, Howard liked to stand near midcourt observing the flow of activity around him. He struck a familiar pose with one arm folded across his chest and the other extended upward with two fingers resting against his chin, exuding a professor-like demeanor. He measured his words, but when he had something to say, players listened, knowing intuitively that whatever he told them would likely help their performance.

Among the boys trying out in 1970 were two newcomers from the Nicholtown community. James Brooks and Jack Taylor lived a couple of blocks from each other, and both carried a significant amount of street credibility among Nicholtown's basketball playing youth.

Taylor was only a ninth-grader and after desegregation was assigned to Northwood Junior High in the Wade Hampton district. At the time, ninth-graders were allowed to try out for varsity sports at their future high schools. Taylor was physically mature, standing 6'3" and weighing a sturdy 180 pounds. He possessed a strong upper body, catlike quickness and explosive leaping ability. He could handle the ball like a guard, but he also had the physical assets that gave him a presence around the basket.

As an eighth-grader, Taylor had been attending Beck Junior High and played on its junior varsity team prior to integration. Clyde Mayes had played with Taylor on the Nicholtown playgrounds, and word quickly got back to Coach Ross to keep an eye on this up-and-coming future General. Taylor immediately impressed Ross and Howard during tryouts with his advanced skills, and the two coaches were greatly encouraged at the realization that the gifted Taylor would be a part of the Wade Hampton program for the next four years.

Brooks transferred to Wade Hampton from Beck as a 10th-grader in February 1970 as part of the school district's desegregation plan.

He had not participated on the basketball team at Beck because he said he failed to get his insurance form completed in time for try-outs. Most of his basketball playing was thus limited to neighborhood pickup games. Like Taylor, Brooks was blessed with an athletic 6'3" frame. He had enormous hands, which allowed him to palm a basketball with ease, and he possessed the best leaping ability of any of the boys hoping to make the team. In tryouts, Brooks established himself as a voracious rebounder, and Ross and Howard knew his skills would greatly complement Clyde Mayes around the basket.

Brooks was quick to flash a broad grin and had a friendly personality. Immediately, he was well liked by his teammates and the student body. Everybody knew him as "Big O," a nickname he pinned on himself on the playgrounds of Nicholtown.

"One day, we were playing in the neighborhood, and everybody started talking about their favorite pro player," Brooks recalled. "One guy said he was 'Clyde' Frazier of the Knicks, so I took up the name

of my favorite player, Oscar Robertson, or 'Big O.' I really liked the way he played the game." At the end of tryouts, Ross typed a list of the names of the 15 boys who had made the team. He taped it inside a glass window in the coaches' office within the locker room. The names were listed in alphabetical order: Doug Abrams, Bud Asbury,

James "Big O" Brooks takes aim on a free-throw attempt. *(Photo courtesy of the* Trevilian, *1972 Wade Hampton High School yearbook)*

203

Johnny Ayers, James Brooks, Charlie Carter, Larry Dogan, Bobby
Estes, Frank Fitzgerald, Clyde Mayes, Norman MacDonald, Will
McNamara, Paul Myers, Steve Phillips, Billy Spink and Jack Taylor.

Ayers, Estes, MacDonald, Mayes, Myers, McNamara and Spink
were returnees from the 1970 state championship team. Abrams,
Asbury and Phillips moved up from the previous year's 13-8 junior

The 1970-71 Wade Hampton Basketball Team: First Row: Billy Spink (left),
Doug Abrams, Charlie Carter, Bobby Estes and Larry Dogan; Second Row:
Johnny Ayers (left), Norman MacDonald, Frank Fitzgerald, Buddy Asbury
and Steve Phillips; Third Row: Will McNamara, (left), Paul Myers, Clyde
Mayes, Jack Taylor and James Brooks *(Photo courtesy of Kelly Ross)*

varsity team. Frank Fitzgerald, a member of the 1969-70 team for a portion of the year, rejoined the squad, and Charlie Carter, a bruising junior football player, also made the team. Later, Ayers dropped off the team to have surgery to repair a deviated septum, and 6'8" junior Larry Dodgens was added to roster.

High school athletic budgets were always tight and fell second in line to the more popular sport of football, but the success of Wade Hampton's basketball team warranted a financial investment. The team replaced their old white semi-satin, belt-buckled home uniforms with new ones made from stretch polyester. The white jerseys were trimmed in red and black, with the historical gray removed from the school colors. It was a subtle move away from the school's link to the Confederacy and one that would continue into modern times.

In 1959, when Vince Lombardi took over as head coach of the NFL's Green Bay Packers, he vowed to change the losing culture of their organization. He believed that every detail, including how a team dressed, had an impact on its ability to create a winning environment. He implemented a dress code for road trips that included ties and shiny new green Packers blazers that Lombardi agreed to purchase out of his own pocket as a personal demonstration of his commitment to the team. Lombardi said, "If we are going to be winners, we have to start looking, acting and feeling like winners."

After the 1970 state championship season, booster club donations funded the purchase of matching red blazers for each player and coach of the Wade Hampton basketball team. The blazers included a gray school logo on the breast pocket, and Generals basketball players were required to wear them with a tie on all road trips. It was a practice that continued for the next seven seasons of Wade Hampton basketball.

Wade Hampton opened the 1970-71 season at home on Friday night, December 4, against T.L. Hanna. The Yellow Jackets' high-scoring guard Terrell Suit had graduated and was playing on the freshman team at Clemson, but they still had 6'7" center Barry Isom and were expected to provide an early season test for the Generals. Missing from the Generals' lineup was Norman MacDonald, who was playing in the Shrine Bowl football game in Charlotte the following day.

Ross started four seniors in the opener: Mayes, Spink, Ayers and McNamara—along with freshman Jack Taylor. The Generals played sluggishly in the first half and held a narrow 21-17 lead. Prior to the season, *Coach and Athlete Magazine* ranked the Generals as the 23rd best high school team in the country, but their first half play was in no way worthy of such a lofty ranking. In the locker room, Coach Ross chastised his team for its lackadaisical play and reminded the players that because they were the defending state champs, they could expect to see everyone's best effort this season. In the second half, the Generals responded to Ross's pep talk and took control of the game, cruising to a 48-33 win. Mayes led Wade Hampton with 16 points, and Spink added 13.

MacDonald said he got a little worried when Assistant Coach Howard told him in math class one day, "This new kid James Brooks might just take your starting position." That fear was squelched when Ross found MacDonald the Monday after the Shrine Bowl and quickly informed him he was counting on his leadership, and he would be back in the starting lineup in the team's second game against Greenwood on Wednesday.

The Greenwood game was part of a high school doubleheader

played in Memorial Auditorium in Downtown Greenville. Officials at the auditorium put together a plan in 1970 whereby several of the area's high school teams played their games in the spacious 6,500-seat arena. Wade Hampton was scheduled to play 14 of its 21 regular-season games there. While not mentioned publicly, it is likely that in the wake of the integration of Greenville County schools, the auditorium was seen as a safer and more controllable environment to play area high school basketball games.

Midway through the basketball season, Lloyd Kelly, scheduling director at the auditorium told *The Greenville News*: "There has been no trouble here this season. And everyone appreciates the sportsmanship shown by the fans. Trouble can be eliminated here because the people are not as close together, and if there should be, we are prepared for it."

Memorial Auditorium opened in December of 1958 and was located on the corner of East North and Church Streets. It was constructed at a cost of $2 million and dedicated to the community's veterans from all wars. Locals referred to it as "the big brown box" in reference to its brown brick, boxy exterior structure. Over the next four decades, it served as a cultural and social center for the Greenville community.

The auditorium became a popular venue for many top musical acts including Ray Charles, Chicago, Three Dog Night and Lynyrd Skynyrd. The rock group Kiss appeared there four times between 1988 and 1992. The largest crowd ever to attend an event at the auditorium, 7,301 fans, came to see Hootie and the Blowfish on December 29, 1994. The auditorium was also home to the Miss South Carolina Pageant from 1958 to 1995.

Monday nights at the auditorium were reserved for Mid-Atlantic

Wrestling, and capacity crowds came to see icons such as Ric Flair, Johnny Weaver, Gene and Ole Anderson, Rufus R. Jones, Andre the Giant and Wahoo McDaniel. Furman University also utilized the facility as its home basketball court from 1958 to 1997, and the Harlem Globetrotters made an annual visit to the Greenville arena.

Each March, the auditorium hosted the Southern Textile Basketball Tournament. The Class A and B divisions of the tournament featured players who worked at local textile mills and other area businesses. The Open Division teams were comprised of college players and historically attracted many top stars including University of North Carolina All-American Billy Cunningham, South Carolina's All-American John Roche and Clemson's future NBA player 7'1" Wayne "Tree" Rollins. The C Division featured high school players and past participants including NBA Hall of Famer "Pistol" Pete Maravich and 2004 NBA Most Valuable Player Kevin Garnett.

On the afternoon of April 30, 1967, Martin Luther King Jr. spoke to an audience of 3,500 in the auditorium as part of a meeting of the Southern Christian Leadership Conference. In his message, King acknowledged the severity of situations facing blacks in the United States. While many were taking desperate actions, he stressed, "Nonviolence is still the best path to achieving civil rights." Less than a year later, King was assassinated outside his hotel room in Memphis, Tennessee.

The Wade Hampton basketball team followed a standard routine for games at the auditorium. They boarded a bus in the athletic parking lot at Wade Hampton for a short four-mile trip downtown. The team was dropped off at the building's back entrance where players walked down a concrete stairway into a maze of underground dressing rooms. Each room contained a few folding chairs and a six-foot folding table that was used as a makeshift trainer's table.

Fans at the auditorium enjoyed a spacious and comfortable experience. Approximately five rows of folding chairs lined the sides of the court with another 10-12 rows behind each basket. The preferred seating was in the oval shaped first balcony that featured green cushioned seats with wooden armrests. The very best seats were on the sides of the court in the first row of the balcony. These seats were about 20 feet from the playing surface and allowed rowdy fans a chance to hang over the balcony railing while they yelled at referees or opposing teams as they ran up and down the court. As fans entered the building, they were quickly enticed by the aroma of freshly popped popcorn. The popcorn was served in green and white cardboard cylinders. After eating the popcorn, younger fans typically knocked out the bottoms of the cylinders and used them as homemade megaphones.

The basketball playing surface at the auditorium was a portable wooden floor. Most players said they could jump an extra couple of inches off the springy surface and were willing to put up with the court's numerous "dead spots" in exchange for the improved leaping ability. Behind each portable basket was a large open space, which greatly affected the depth perception of a shooter. Players visiting the auditorium for the first time were prone to launch "air balls" until they adjusted to the unfamiliar and cavernous backdrop. For Wade Hampton's 1970-71 season, the auditorium became a "home away from home" where victories were plentiful and losses nonexistent.

Ross juggled his starting lineup for the Greenwood game, reinserting the previous year's starters, Bobby Estes at guard and MacDonald at forward. This starting lineup of Mayes, MacDonald, Spink, Estes and Taylor was one that Ross would stick with for the majority

The 6,500-seat Greenville Memorial Auditorium
(Photo courtesy of midatlanticwrestling.net)

of the season.

The Generals' offense clicked against Greenwood as they rolled to an easy 72-43 win. All five starters scored in double figures with Mayes leading the way with 21. Estes had 12, and MacDonald, Taylor and Spink each scored 10. Ross was able to play all 15 of his players in the lopsided victory.

The following Saturday, the Generals were part of another high school doubleheader at the auditorium as they faced Parker. The Golden Tornadoes had lost standout Gary Pittman from the previous season's 21-3 team. Larry Wall, a recent graduate of High Point College and a young high school coach from Broadway, North Carolina, took over the coaching responsibilities at Parker from Coach Bob Winters, who had accepted a job as an assistant coach at the College of Charleston.

Parker attempted to neutralize the Generals' potent offense by slowing the tempo. In a low-scoring affair, Wade Hampton held off the Golden Tornadoes 47-37, as Mayes led all scorers with 26 points.

The Generals stood at 3-0 and were the favorites to win the upcoming Greenville County Invitational Christmas Tournament.

In the opening round of the annual Christmas tournament, the Generals defeated defending champion J.L. Mann 52-41 to set up a semifinal match-up with Carolina High. The Trojans were coached by Louie Golden, who had landed at Carolina after the closing of Beck High School the previous year. The game was an emotional one for Golden, who had to coach against his former star pupil, Clyde Mayes. Golden also faced other former Beck players when he played against Greenville and J.L. Mann.

When asked by reporter Parks Morgan of *The Greenville News* about his feelings with respect to competing against his former pupils, Golden said, "It's good to see that they are still playing, that they have gone to different schools and have made the adjustments with new coaches and new teams, but sometimes I look back and say 'Wow! See what a team I could have had.'"

Mayes showed no mercy to his former mentor and coach as he dominated the game against Carolina, scoring 28 points and leading the Generals to a 61-45 victory. Greenville High also won its semifinal game, which meant Wade Hampton would face its archrival in the tourney's championship.

Admission to the Saturday night championship match-up was $1.50 for adults and $1.25 for students, and more than 2,000 fans showed up for the 9 p.m. game to see Mayes and Greenville's Clyde Agnew square off in what would be the first of five "Battles of the Clydes" during the 1970-71 season. Greenville came into the game 4-1 and was led by the 6'6" Agnew, who had added 20 pounds of muscle to his frame over the summer. Sharpshooting guard Randy Miller and 6'4" forward Mike Smith were also key contributors for

Coach Smith Danielson's Red Raiders.

Wade Hampton led by 10 at the half and was up 13 at the end of the third quarter before the Raiders used an all-out full court press to force several Generals turnovers. Greenville pulled within six late in the game, but Wade Hampton held on to secure a 68-62 win. Mayes, who sat out much of the game in foul trouble and collected his fifth foul with two minutes to play, led all scorers with 21 points. Agnew scored 18 and outrebounded Mayes 17-13.

MacDonald and Spink added 15 each, and Bobby Estes scored 11. James Brooks was the only reserve Ross played in the game, beginning a season-long pattern of substituting rarely in close games. Mayes was named the most valuable player of the tournament, and MacDonald joined him on the all-tournament team.

"It was a little easier at first than I expected. And near the end, it was a little harder than I thought it would be," Coach Ross commented after the game. "We went in using a 1-2-2 offense against them and a match-up zone defense. The offense was effective, but they did manage to put pressure on us toward the end without Clyde in there.

Moments after winning the championship in the 1970 Greenville County Invitational Christmas Tournament, Coach Johnny Ross and Assistant Coach Lynn Howard smile as they admire their team's trophy. *(Photo courtesy of the* Trevilian, *1971 Wade Hampton High School yearbook)*

Their good outside shooting kept our defense from being as effective as it has been."

The Generals entered the Christmas break 6-0, and Ross was pleased with the way his team was beginning to gel. Defensively, Ross continued to rely on the match-up zone, switching periodically to a man-to-man defense when needed. His offensive approach remained simple—get the ball inside to Mayes.

"We all knew our job was to get the ball in to Clyde," teammate Jack Taylor recalled. When Mayes received a pass on the block, he was virtually unstoppable. A quick drop step followed by a layup or a short turnaround bank shot were high percentage shots for the Generals' center. Ross reserved his harshest reprimands for players who elected to loft long-range jumpers in lieu of dropping the ball inside to Mayes. Ross's philosophy was difficult to swallow for some of the team's better shooters such as Estes.

"I can remember being told specifically not to shoot the ball," Estes said. "I remember one game at Parker where I was gun-shy to take a 10-footer for fear [Ross] might pull me out of the game. We all had to accept the role we were being asked to play."

An offensive strategy that centered around making one player the focal point required first that this star player be well liked by his teammates. Players will not pass the ball to a self-centered glory hound. Mayes' humility and overall affable personality made this possible, along with a supporting cast of teammates who prioritized winning above their own individual statistics.

After the Christmas break, the Generals defeated Easley, Carolina and J.L. Mann to bring their record to 9-0 as they prepared for their second match-up against Greenville on Friday night, January 15, at the auditorium. Once again, a large crowd of nearly 2,000 fans showed up to witness the rivalry game.

Coach Ross knew the best chance Greenville would have against his team would result from Mayes sitting out due to foul trouble. The most memorable moment in any game for Ross was when his friend and longtime Generals' scorekeeper Frank Sutherland caught Ross's attention and held up three or four fingers as he pointed toward Mayes. In an effort to reduce Mayes' fouls, Ross assigned the 6'1" MacDonald to cover Greenville's Agnew. While he gave up five inches in height, MacDonald used his quickness and anticipation skills to harass Agnew throughout the game.

Frustrated by MacDonald's success and in keeping with the intensity of the rivalry between the two schools, the Greenville cheerleaders attempted to unnerve the Generals' senior leader. As MacDonald lined up to shoot a free throw, the Red Raiders' cheerleaders were positioned on the baseline under the Generals' basket and began singing the lyrics to a popular song from the 1960s by Sue Thompson entitled "Norman." Norman, ooh, ooh, ooh, ooh, ooh, ooh, ooh, ooh…MacDonald said the harassment made him smile but did not keep him from stepping to the foul line and sinking both of his free-throw shots. Ross's strategy worked, as Mayes was able to play most of the game and scored 28 points and hauled in 23 rebounds. The aggressive Generals' defense forced 13 Red Raider turnovers as Wade Hampton rolled to a surprisingly easy 87-60 win. "I think we played our best game of the season," a pleased Coach Ross said after the game.

A 20-point win over Greer put the Generals at 11-0 overall and 7-0 in the conference headed into a road match-up against Hanna, a team they had beaten in the season opener. The Generals held a slim four-point margin at the half and moved out to a commanding

Norman MacDonald (41) scores on a layup in a game in Memorial Auditorium during the 1970-71 season. *(Photo courtesy of Norman MacDonald)*

15-point lead late in the third quarter before suffering their biggest setback of the season.

Late in the game, point guard Billy Spink dove toward the sideline in an attempt to retrieve a loose ball. His body slid along the floor, and he tried to brace himself with his left hand, which by that time had slid underneath the wooden bleachers. His hand rammed against the bleacher support, and he recalled "hearing something snap." Spink suffered a broken bone in his left hand and was sidelined indefinitely. Back-up guards Steve Phillips and Doug Abrams alternated at point guard for the rest of the game. Spink was the quarterback of the Generals' attack; once he left the lineup, their offense was out of sync, but they still managed to hold on for the 58-49 win.

After the Hanna game, Ross experimented in practice with a number of combinations in an attempt to make up for the loss of his floor leader. For the previous two seasons, Spink was Ross's "coach on the floor," and it was nearly impossible to compensate for the leadership void created by his absence.

Abrams, who played behind Spink at point guard, said of his teammate: "Physically, Billy was this little, short wide guy with a short stride, but he was the guy who ran the team. His intellect and his character are what made him so good. When you needed somebody to make a big play, he was the guy who had the coolness under pressure."

The Generals traveled to Greenwood for their first contest without Spink in the lineup. Wade Hampton had destroyed Greenwood 72-43 earlier in the year, and even without Spink, the team was confident they could secure another easy win.

Prior to the game, the players sat on benches in the locker room as they waited for Ross to deliver his final pregame instructions. Mac-Donald recalled that he and Will McNamara began flicking pieces of rolled up athletic tape at each other and also threw some of the pieces at the ceiling in an effort to get them to stick. When Coach Ross entered the room, he sensed their lackadaisical attitude and scolded them directly for their playfulness. As Ross was going over the game plan, MacDonald and his teammates struggled not to burst into laughter when a piece of the tape broke loose from the ceiling and drifted onto the top of Ross's balding head.

The Generals lack of pregame focus spilled onto the court where the Greenwood players took advantage of their overconfident opponents. Recognizing they were without their starting point guard,

Greenwood applied full court pressure to the less experienced Wade Hampton guards, which disrupted the normal cohesiveness of the Generals' offense. The game was knotted at 60 in the fourth quarter, and Greenwood converted on eight of nine free throws down the stretch to secure the upset win and end Wade Hampton's hopes of an undefeated season. Losing was a new experience for Ross's team, and an unfamiliar silence filled the Generals' bus as it traveled down S.C. Highway 25 for what was a very somber 55-mile ride back to Greenville.

Ross continued to try different combinations to make up for the absence of Spink, finally inserting Brooks as the fifth starter and relying on Estes to trigger the offensive attack. Mayes and MacDonald stepped forward as senior leaders and began to play with a renewed sense of passion. Over the next six games with Spink out of the starting lineup, the two veteran players averaged 22 and 18 points respectively as Wade Hampton reeled off six

Clyde Mayes (55) snares a rebound away from Parker's Daryl Wilder (52) in a game at Parker on February 2, 1971. *(Photo courtesy of the* Parkerscope, *1971 Parker High School yearbook)*

217

straight wins, including their third of the year over archrival Greenville. The win over Greenville upped Wade Hampton's overall record to 18-1 and gave them a perfect 16-0 conference mark and a top seed in the upcoming Region II 4A tournament. The region tournament was played at T.L. Hanna High in its new gymnasium, which had a seating capacity of nearly 3,000. In the opening round, Wade Hampton played last-place Easley, a team it had beaten handily in two regular season games. In his pregame message, Ross told his team that Easley did not have a player who could stop Mayes. Once again, he emphatically instructed his team to pass the ball inside to Mayes on every offensive possession and let its big man operate on the weaker Easley post players. The results of Ross's strategy led to Mayes' most dominant offensive performance of the year, as he scored a school-record 40 points and tied a record with 33 rebounds. The following night, Wade Hampton defeated Louie Golden's Carolina Trojans 73-50, setting up their fourth game of the season with Greenville in the tournament final.

Wade Hampton was already guaranteed a spot in the upper state playoffs by virtue of winning the regular season championship. Greenville also had earned the right to advance to the playoffs, meaning their match-up in the region tourney final was only for "bragging rights."

"I remember Coach Ross telling us before the game that we were going to the state playoffs again and that this game did not matter," Norman MacDonald recalled. Perhaps Ross was hoping his message would relieve some of the pressure his defending state championship team carried with them to every game.

The reaction to his message, however, was that his team played its least inspired basketball of the season. Wade Hampton also experienced one of its poorest shooting nights of the year, connecting on only 19 of 58 field goal attempts. As a foreshadowing of the game's eventual outcome, Greenville's Randy Miller sank a desperation shot from beyond the half court line at the end of the first half to knot the score at 26.

Greenville had the ball with 13 seconds remaining, trailing by a point when they called a timeout. Ross told his team to expect that Greenville would try to get the ball to their star Clyde Agnew for the final shot. Ross put his team in a man-to-man defense with Mayes assigned to Agnew, but he told MacDonald to double team Agnew as soon as he touched the ball. As expected, Greenville ran a play for Agnew, and MacDonald immediately moved toward Agnew for the double team, leaving his man David Pruitt open on the perimeter. Agnew sensed the double team and tossed the ball to the open Pruitt, who lofted a 20-foot shot that rattled around the rim before dropping in. Wade Hampton turned the ball over in a desperate attempt for a final score, and Clyde Agnew sank a free throw to give the Raiders the 45-43 upset over their archrival.

After the game, sensing that the win gave his team a boost of needed confidence, a jubilant Greenville Coach Smith Danielson said, "We waited a long time for this one. We did what we had to do."

Ross, perhaps realizing that he had not prepared his team properly for the match-up, was brief in his postgame remarks saying, "Greenville played well. We didn't. That's all I have to say."

The Upper State Tournament was scheduled for the following Thursday through Saturday nights at Spartanburg High's Red Dobson Gymnasium, the venue where Wade Hampton captured the state title the previous March. Both Wade Hampton and Greenville drew first-round byes with Wade Hampton scheduled to play the winner of the Spartanburg and Columbia game and Greenville facing the winner of Byrnes and Greenwood. Spartanburg won its opener, setting up Wade Hampton's semifinal match-up against the hometown Vikings.

Spartanburg held an impressive 23-2 record and were champions of Region III 4A. The Vikings featured a high-powered offense averaging more than 80 points and were led by All-American guard Doug Lowe. Standing only 5'9", Lowe was a scoring machine, averaging 24 points. Early in the season, he set the school's single-game scoring record when he tossed in 51 points. Lowe later played at Wofford College, and in 1979, he became the head boys basketball coach at Spartanburg High, a position he held for 31 years, during which time he amassed a 626-212 record, won 19 region titles, made four state final appearances and won one 4A title. In 2014, the court in the Red Dobson Gymnasium was named in his honor.

The game of basketball through the 1960s and '70s was dominated by big men. Bill Russell, Wilt Chamberlain and Kareem Abdul-Jabbar set the standard for post players during an era where there was no 3-point shot, and the success of teams hinged heavily upon having a dominant center. Many basketball coaches during this era viewed outside shooting similar to the way legendary Alabama football coach Bear Bryant viewed the forward pass, seeing it only as a necessary evil.

Ross's strategy for a second run at a state title maximized the use of his star center. Now more than ever, he would emphasize to his players that Mayes was the most dominant high school basketball player in South Carolina, and they were going to rely heavily on him to defeat every opponent that stood in their way.

Ross confidently told his team before the Spartanburg game that

Lowe would "get his points," but there was no way Spartanburg could stop the powerful inside game of Mayes. By forcing the ball inside, Ross knew his team would take higher percentage shots, and it would maintain a rebounding advantage. When executed properly, Ross's strategy had proven to be a guaranteed formula for success.

A standing-room-only crowed filled Red Dobson Gymnasium for the 8:30 p.m. game between Wade Hampton and Spartanburg. The Generals bought into Ross's strategy and fed their big man at every opportunity. Mayes quickly took over the game, scoring eight of Wade Hampton's first 10 points on his way to 22 in the first half. Wade Hampton never trailed and rolled to a surprisingly easy 80-67 win.

Mayes led all scorers with 35, and MacDonald scored 15, while Estes continued his excellent play in the postseason, scoring 12 and leading an inspired defensive effort that frustrated Spartanburg's Lowe as he scored only 14 and fouled out with 5:44 to play. James Brooks was the lone substitute Ross used.

Spartanburg's head coach Fred Fraley summed up the game this way: "It was just a matter of too much Mayes. Our game plan was to try to stop Mayes, but when they got the ball inside to him, there was nothing we could do."

Greenville, playing by far its best basketball of the season, routed Byrnes 57-35 in the semifinals, setting up its fifth and final match-up with Wade Hampton. Ross knew how to beat Greenville—get the ball inside to Mayes, keep Mayes out of foul trouble and neutralize as much as possible Greenville's Agnew. On the other side, Coach Smith Danielson knew the key to stopping Wade Hampton was to somehow hold Mayes in check.

Ross assigned MacDonald and Jack Taylor to take turns guarding

Agnew in an effort to limit Mayes' fouls. MacDonald and Taylor aggravated Agnew throughout the game, holding him to only 12 points and thus keeping the Raider offense out of sync.

Clyde Mayes (55) pulls down a rebound against Greenville High in the Upper State finals at Red Dobson Gymnasium in Spartanburg. Greenville's David Pruitt looks on in the background. *(Photo courtesy of the* Trevilian, *1971 Wade Hampton High School yearbook)*

Wade Hampton led 28-23 at the half and went on a 13-2 third-quarter run that put the game out of reach. Spink played an excellent all-around game, and the outside shooting of Estes and Taylor helped open up the Generals' offense when the Raiders attempted to pack their defense inside against Mayes.

"I sincerely think five is a gracious plenty," Ross said after the victory. "We have had five good games with Greenville, and to beat them four out of five is good enough for us."

Mayes was the leading scorer with 20 points despite sitting out much of the second half in foul trouble. Spink added 18, including eight of eight free throws down the stretch, and Taylor contributed 11. Once again, Ross elected to use Brooks as his lone substitute. Mayes, MacDonald and Spink were named to the 10-person all-tournament team.

Reese Fant covered the Upper State final game for *The Greenville News*. Afterward, he asked Mayes what it felt like to be going to the state final for the second year in a row. While well-intended, Fant's question failed in the moment to give credit to the entirety of Mayes' high school career.

"Sir, I have already been three straight years. This will be my fourth year," Mayes said respectfully drawing recognition to the fact that as a ninth and 10th-grader at Beck High School, he played for Coach Louie Golden's teams in state 3A finals in the black high school league.

Both of those state championship games for Beck were played in relative obscurity on the campus of South Carolina State University in Orangeburg. Media coverage of the games was scant, and for many like Fant they were a forgotten part of Mayes' impressive high school career. However, on the Saturday following the 1971 Upper

State Championship, Mayes and his Wade Hampton teammates were headed to play on the state's biggest stage, Columbia's 12,401-seat Carolina Coliseum. Every major media outlet in the state would be on hand to cover the game.

12
Back-to-Back

Winning takes talent; to repeat takes character.

John Wooden

Fifty-two schools competed in Class 4A high school basketball in South Carolina during the 1970-71 season. By the end of February, only two teams remained—Wade Hampton and Dreher of Columbia. Their championship match-up was set for Saturday, March 6, at 9:15 p.m. in Columbia's Carolina Coliseum.

Neither team knew much about the other as they were playing in an era when game films and advance scouting were almost nonexistent. Both coaching staffs had to piece together a game strategy based on information derived from their respective network of contacts, along with knowledge gained from reading press clippings and hearing anecdotal stories.

Dreher entered the game 26-1 as regular season and tournament champions of Region IV 4A. The previous Saturday, they had defeated Middleton to win the Lower State championship. The Blue Devils were coached by 33-year-old Dixon Owens, a 1962 graduate of Duke University. Owens was a catcher on Duke's 1961 baseball team that won the ACC championship and finished fifth in the College World Series. In his junior and senior years, Owens served as a student assistant coach for Duke's freshman basketball team. After graduating from Duke, he worked in the school's physical education department and remained as a part-time assistant for the freshman basketball team, working for three years alongside Duke's freshman coach, 33-year-old Chuck Daly. After six years as an assistant at Duke, Daly launched a highly successful collegiate and professional head coaching career that included winning back-to-back NBA championships with the Detroit Pistons and becoming the coach of the first U.S. Olympic Dream team in 1992. Owens took the head basketball coaching job at Dreher in 1965, a position he held for the next 23 years.

The star of Dreher's team was Alexander English, a slender 6'6" junior with silky smooth moves around the basket. He was averaging 22 points and 15.5 rebounds a game and scored 35 against Middleton in the Upper State championship. Mike Hembree was a journalism student at the University of South Carolina in 1971 and also worked full time as a sportswriter with *The State* newspaper, covering prep sports in the Midlands. He had seen English play several times.

"English was different from any other prep player I had seen in the state," Hembree recalled. "He was polished, played with great finesse and had a very soft jumper from inside of 15 feet."

After graduating from Dreher, English signed to play for Coach Frank McGuire at the University of South Carolina. In announcing English's signing with USC, McGuire said, "He's certainly one of the best high school players in the entire country. He can play with anyone, anywhere." English started every game in his four years at USC and led the Gamecocks to a couple of NCAA tournament appearances and one NIT showing, while also earning All-America honors. His number, 22, is one of five Gamecock basketball jersey numbers that have been retired.

English was selected in the second round of the 1976 NBA Draft by the Milwaukee Bucks where he spent two years, followed by two years with the Indiana Pacers, before landing in Denver where he played the next 11 years. At Denver, English was an eight-time NBA All-Star and became the all-time leading scorer in Nuggets' history. English was elected to the Naismith Basketball Hall of Fame in 1997.

English grew up in humble surroundings in the Valley Park section of Columbia and learned to play basketball on neighborhood playgrounds similar to the ones in Greenville's Nicholtown where Clyde Mayes honed his basketball skills. English was quiet and reserved, yet by the time he reached high school, like Mayes, he had emerged as an influential leader on and off the court.

The State's Bob Gillespie wrote an in-depth article that was published the day English was inducted into the National Basketball Hall of Fame in 1997. Included in Gillespie's story were the following insights from Sue Elliott, English's academic counselor at Dreher, and Sammy Adams, a Dreher teammate and lifelong friend.

"Every once in a while, when you work with youngsters, special people come along," Elliott said in the interview with Gillespie. "Something drew me to him, made me want to protect him from the world…He was one of those people who are aware of what's going on with others around him. We'd talk about why people hurt other people. Alex was always concerned about the less fortunate."

Adams shared a story from their old neighborhood that validated Elliott's claim about English's concern for others.

"In Valley Park, there was this guy, a 'wino,' who everyone would tell to get on, but Alex would take the guy home, treat him like anyone else, talk to him, try to understand his problem," Adams said.

Elliott and Adams recalled a race riot that closed Dreher High School in March of 1972, in which, Elliott said English gathered black students in the gymnasium and "preached calm." Adams also remembered English's reaction to the outbreak: "When the incident broke out, some wanted to fight. Alex told everyone, 'Let's reason this out.'"

Ongoing racial tension stemming from school desegregation in the Columbia area, along with several fights and skirmishes that occurred at sporting events during this time, led Columbia area school leaders to require all high schools to play the majority of their 1970-71 regular season basketball games in the afternoon. As a result, many of Dreher's games were played in front of sparse crowds. However, for the state championship game, Dreher would play in "prime time" in Carolina Coliseum, the state's newest and largest sports venue.

Construction of the coliseum was completed in 1968 at a cost of $7 million. The coliseum complex spread across 8.5 acres at the corner of Assembly and Blossom Streets, and in addition to the basketball arena, it included more than 500 underground offices and classrooms that served principally as the home of the University of South Carolina School of Journalism and College of General Studies.

The coliseum quickly became known as "The House that Frank Built" in recognition of McGuire's influence on its construction. With a reputation as one of the most well-known and successful basketball coaches in the country, McGuire arrived in Columbia in 1964. A native of New York City, he was the youngest of 13 children in an Irish-American family. He was a four-sport standout at St. John's University and spent 11 years coaching and teaching history at St. Francis Xavier High School in Manhattan before becoming a collegiate coach at St. John's. In five years at St. John's, McGuire was 67-25 and led his 1952 team to the NCAA final. McGuire also coached the St. John's baseball team and took it to the College World

Series in 1949.

McGuire left St. John's after the 1952 season to become the head coach at the University of North Carolina in Chapel Hill. The move south was influenced in part by his desire to get his 1-year-old son Frankie, who was afflicted with cerebral palsy, to a more conducive climate. His 1957 UNC team completed a 32-0 season that included a double-overtime win over the Kansas Jayhawks in the national championship game. Ten of the 13 players on UNC's championship team were from the New York metro area.

After nine years in Chapel Hill, McGuire became the head coach and general manager of the Philadelphia Warriors of the NBA. The Warriors' star player was the former University of Kansas star, 7'1" Wilt Chamberlain. McGuire and Chamberlain developed a respectful and effective working relationship during a season in which Chamberlain set an NBA single-season scoring record, averaging 50.4 points per game and establishing the single-game scoring record with 100 points against the New York Knicks. At the end of the season, the Warriors announced they were moving to San Francisco and rather than move his family west, McGuire resigned and spent two years away from coaching.

On March 13, 1964, the 47-year-old McGuire was named the head basketball coach and associate athletic director at South Carolina. Prior to McGuire's arrival, the Gamecocks' basketball team had posted only two winning seasons over the previous 12. Since becoming founding members of the Atlantic Coast Conference in 1953, the Gamecocks had failed to have a winning record against conference opponents. Once again, McGuire capitalized on his deep New York City connections and began to lure some of New York's top basketball talent to Columbia. Within five years in Columbia, McGuire turned South Carolina into a national basketball powerhouse and had his Gamecock teams ranked among the nation's elite.

Part of convincing McGuire to accept the coaching position at USC was the school's promise to build a new basketball arena. The Gamecocks were playing in an outdated barn-box known as Carolina Fieldhouse. Built in 1927, the Fieldhouse seated only 3,200 and was not suited for the championship caliber of basketball that Mc-Guire intended to bring to USC.

McGuire's 1968-69 team included a class of blue-chip recruits and was expected to contend for the ACC championship. The initial plans were for the team to begin its season in the old Fieldhouse and move to the new coliseum once it was completed somewhere in the middle of the season. However, a fire destroyed the Fieldhouse in the spring of 1968, forcing the urgent need to complete construction of the coliseum in time for the Gamecocks' first game.

Rumors spread that McGuire was responsible for starting the fire in order to expedite the completion of the coliseum in time for the 1968 season opener. If true, it was a secret the legendary coach took with him when he passed away in 1994. The Gamecocks opened the coliseum on the evening of November 30, 1968, with a 51-49 victory over Auburn.

Reportedly, McGuire insisted that the seating capacity at the coliseum exceed the largest arena in the ACC, which, at the time, was NC State's Reynolds Coliseum with 12,400 seats. Carolina Coliseum's final basketball seating capacity was officially established at 12,401.

The coliseum's garnet-colored cushioned seats extended straight up to the roof with no balconies or structural support columns blocking a fan's sight lines. The most apt description of the seating in the coliseum was "steep." Fans in the upper sections of the arena said they felt that if they stood up too quickly, they might topple out of their seats and land at center court. The lighting in the arena was focused on the playing surface, and seating areas were darkened, giving a theatrical effect.

The basketball-playing floor of the coliseum was a rubberized inch-thick surface that was marketed by the 3M Company in the '70s under the brand name of "tartan." It was an indestructible multi-purpose floor that was best described as a basketball version of Astro-Turf™. One unusual aspect of the floor was that it muffled the sound of a bouncing basketball, which first-time players said made the simple task of dribbling a new and confounding experience at times.

Wade Hampton arrived in Columbia on Saturday afternoon and checked into the Golden Eagle Motor Inn at the corner of Main and Elmwood Streets, a few blocks north of the coliseum. Players gathered for a pregame meal and then lounged in their rooms until it was time for a short bus ride to the coliseum. The 4A championship game was the last of six to be played on that day and the "estimated" tip-off time was 9:15 p.m.

After sitting through the first half of the 3A championship game between Garrett of Charleston and York, the Generals were escorted to one of the many dressing rooms located in the recesses of the coliseum. They were the visiting team and dressed in their old red uniforms that were threadbare in places and outdated. Freshman Jack Taylor went through his normal pregame ritual of putting on multiple pairs of socks over his stirrup socks before slipping his feet into his white canvas Converse All Stars. The muscular Taylor had skinny ankles and calves and used the socks to hide his lone physical shortcoming. Clyde Mayes sat in a chair on the opposite side of the dressing room and pulled a red sweatband across his left wrist and put a white one on his right wrist, a lucky combination that had served him well during the past two seasons.

Coach Ross gathered the team and went over a familiar strategy. To no one's surprise, he once again outlined a very simple offensive game plan—get the ball inside to Clyde. Defensively, the goal was to keep Mayes out of foul trouble. Ross told his starters to begin the game in a man-to-man defense and assigned 6'1" Norman MacDonald to cover 6'6" English. Ross told Mayes, who was assigned defensive responsibility for Dreher's 6'6" center Alan Searson, to sag and help MacDonald whenever English received the ball inside. Ross told his boys to expect full-court defensive pressure and an up-tempo pace from the Blue Devils. His final instructions were to "play smart and under control" and not to panic. As in every game Ross coached, he asked his team to circle up, take a knee and recite together the Lord's Prayer as its final act of preparation.

In the Dreher locker room, the Blue Devils dressed in their home white uniforms. Alexander English stretched his trademark white headband around his head to complete his pregame dress protocol. Coach Owens told his team the key to stopping Wade Hampton was to stop Mayes, and he instructed his players to collapse their defense on the Wade Hampton big man whenever he received the ball near the basket. Owens said they would take their chances on other players being able to score, but they were to focus their defensive efforts on stopping Mayes.

After the completion of the state 3A championship game, Wade Hampton and Dreher ran onto the court for their pregame warm-ups. They had less than 20 minutes to get accustomed to the unfamiliar and unique surroundings of the cavernous coliseum.

On Dreher's first possession, players were surprised to see the undersized MacDonald attempting to front English in the low post. One of the Dreher guards quickly lofted the ball inside toward English, but MacDonald, who had been a high jumper on the track team, leaped up and ripped the ball away from English's outstretched arms. On the next two possessions, MacDonald used his quickness to knock away entry passes aimed at English, as he single-handedly frustrated the Blue Devils' offense. Wade Hampton took a 3-0 lead and never trailed in the 32-minute contest.

The spark plug of the Blue Devils' offense was its point guard Sammy Adams. Earlier in the year, Adams was described in *The State* as "an artist at squirming his way inside for layups and a good man on the fast break." Adams, who was averaging 16 points a game, picked up two quick fouls in the first two-and-a-half minutes, forcing him to sit out the remainder of the first quarter. When Adams returned to the floor, Billy Spink lured him into an offensive charging foul, which sent the Blue Devils' floor leader back to the bench for the remainder of the half. Without Adams running their attack, the Blue Devils were out of sync. The contest was tied twice during the first eight minutes, but Mayes started to exert his influence in the second quarter as Wade Hampton moved out to a 31-21 halftime lead.

"The game was kind of like a big heavyweight bout that had lots of hype and anticipation, but then ends rather abruptly in an early round," recalled Mike Hembree of *The State*. "Mayes was such a dominating physical force, and things seemed to go Wade Hampton's way early."

Dreher mounted a furious rally early in the second half, pulling within 34-29 with 5:02 left in the third quarter. The team used a pressing defense to force several turnovers and continued to key its defense on Mayes. While Mayes was drawing the attention of multiple Blue Devil defenders, Jack Taylor was left open, and the 6'3" freshman calmly sank four consecutive shots, including two from long range.

"We pressed Mayes well, especially in the first part of the game. We stayed on him, and they were having a hard time finding him under the basket. Taylor hurt us by hitting those shots when we pulled within five points in the second half," Dreher's Owens told *The State*.

Bobby Estes (31) and Jack Taylor (53) double team Alton Brant (15) of Dreher in the 1971 state championship game at Carolina Coliseum. *(Photo courtesy of the Ross family)*

With five minutes to play in the game, Dreher fought back to within six, but Wade Hampton scored seven consecutive points and moved to a commanding 55-42 lead with 3:21 to play. Mayes, who scored five of those seven on that run, finished the game with 21 points and 19 rebounds.

MacDonald had high praise for his teammate Mayes' performance:

"Clyde played at a different level in that game than any before. It was as if he said, 'This is the most important game in my life so far,' and he played at a higher level to help us achieve our goal of a state championship. He owned the boards at both ends. He had so much more talent than any of us realized."

English sank a free throw with a few seconds remaining, and the two large scoreboards that hung high above the rows of cushioned seats at each end of the coliseum lit up with the final score of 61-53. As the horn sounded, Wade Hampton's players, cheerleaders and fans rushed onto the tartan surface and celebrated the Generals' second consecutive 4A championship.

Point guard Billy Spink scored 14 points, Taylor had 12, MacDonald logged 10 and Bobby Estes added four for the Generals. English led all scorers with 22, while Sammy Adams scored only five in limited playing time. Wade Hampton converted on 19 of 23 free throws while Dreher missed seven of its 12 free-throw attempts. Once again, Ross elected to use James Brooks as his lone substitute in the game. A satisfied and jubilant Coach Ross commented on the overall physical play of the contest.

"This was one of the roughest games we have been in," Ross said. "We are not used to playing against that type of defense. They had the roughest pressing defense I have ever seen. The important thing is that we won, and it sure feels great to be number one for two straight years."

Clyde Mayes leaps high to grab a rebound away from the
outstretched hands of Dreher's Al McEachin (41) in the
state championship game as Jack Taylor (53) looks on.
(Photo courtesy of Kelly Ross)

In 2018, Alexander English was the guest speaker at the press conference, kicking off the South Carolina High School League's basketball championship week. English used a portion of his talk that day
to reflect on the 1971 championship game.

"Clyde Mayes beat me to a pulp in that game. He was just massive. He was big, but he had long arms too. He just took over and

236

controlled the game," English said. "One of the things I learned from playing in that high school state championship game was humility. My team depended on me to be the leader, and he (Mayes) blocked my shot four or five times. It was very frustrating. I wasn't used to that."

Mayes blocked six shots in the game, and English said that it was Mayes' shot blocking that led him to change the release point for his jump shot prior to his senior year in high school, a change that

Clyde Mayes (34) secures a rebound in the 1974 NCAA Tournament game between Furman and South Carolina at The Palestra in Philadelphia. Teammate Craig Lynch (40) and South Carolina's Alex English (22) are nearby.
(Photo courtesy of Furman University Athletics)

helped propel his prolific basketball career. English was known for his accurate midrange jumper. When he shot with his long arms nearly fully extended and utilized a mere flick of the wrists to arc the ball softly toward the basket, he was all but impossible to block.

Three years after the state championship game, Mayes and English faced each other in the first round of the 1974 NCAA Tournament. English and the South Carolina Gamecocks were ranked 10th in the nation and were favored over Mayes and Furman. South Carolina held a 12-point lead early in the second half, but behind the strength of Mayes, Furman rallied to upset the Gamecocks 75-67 in the game played at the historic Palestra in Philadelphia. Mayes finished with 21 points, 16 rebounds and five blocks.

Mayes was selected 22nd overall by the Milwaukee Bucks in 1975, and the Bucks picked English 23rd in the 1976 NBA Draft. The two, however, did not play together professionally as Mayes left the Bucks prior to the start of the 1976-77 season.

———————

The duel between English and Mayes symbolically ushered in a new era of high school sports in the state of South Carolina. Never before had two black athletes garnered such statewide attention in a fully integrated South Carolina High School League championship contest. Never before had two black superstars led historically white high schools on a stage as large as the one in the Carolina Coliseum on the evening of March 6, 1971.

Gone were the days of black high schools competing for separate championships with little or no public recognition from the larger community. Mayes and English pioneered a new era of fully integrated athletic competition within the state and inspired the next generation of young athletes. Mayes and English became the first black athletes at their respective colleges to have their jersey numbers retired. They became the first black athletes from South Carolina to enjoy lengthy and successful professional basketball careers. After their professional careers, both returned to their hometowns and became fixtures in their communities.

———————

It was well past midnight by the time the Generals showered and dressed and made their way back to the Golden Eagle Motor Inn. Despite the late hour, the team's short bus ride to the hotel was filled with rowdy chants and songs in celebration of the victory. Coach Ross sat alongside Assistant Coach Lynn Howard in the front seat holding the Generals' second state championship trophy tightly.

Before the players got off the bus at the Golden Eagle, Ross told them to head directly to their rooms and go to sleep. Breakfast would be ready for them at 8 a.m. in the hotel's restaurant; afterward, they would immediately board the bus for the 100-mile ride back to Greenville.

In an uncommon act of willful disobedience, several of the players sneaked out of their rooms and roamed the streets of Columbia in the wee hours of the morning. It was their attempt to keep the glory of the evening alive. Eventually, the players made it back to their rooms without incident, but any possibility of sleep was lost due to their adrenalin-infused euphoria.

Wade Hampton's final record for the 1970-71 season was 24-2. Six of the seven seniors on the team had been a part of the first two state championships in their school's history. They had just beaten a very talented Dreher team that featured a future Hall of Famer.

Certainly it would be easy to point to the talented Mayes as being singularly responsible for Wade Hampton's back-to-back state championships, and the championships most likely would not have occurred without his skillful play and leadership. Still, competitive sports demonstrate repeatedly that talent alone does not guarantee victory.

Similar to the previous year's state championship team, the 1970-71 version of the Wade Hampton basketball team formed an internal bond. The players had an undeniable chemistry that stemmed from their valuing camaraderie over ego and ultimately accentuated their talent. Off the court, the players became friends. Cultural barriers were crossed, and differences were put aside. The friendships and mutual respect for one another spilled onto the court and provided the intangible quality that is needed to win championships.

Junior backup point guard Doug Abrams was the son of a prominent white Greenville attorney. He had attended a prestigious private school in Greenville prior to coming to Wade Hampton. He lived with his family in a spacious and comfortable home atop Paris Mountain. Abrams' black teammates Jack Taylor and James Brooks grew up in Nicholtown in an environment that was a stark contrast to that of Abrams. Nearly 50 years after playing basketball with them, Abrams recalled with great passion his friendship with Taylor and Brooks.

"We became great friends, and I have so many fond memories of shooting pool with James and Jack at our house and all the good times we enjoyed together," Abrams recalled.

In a post-Civil Rights Era in the Deep South, at a high school named in honor of a Confederate general, the game of basketball became a unifying force between white and black teammates. It propelled a diverse group of young men to play together, to like and respect one another and to become champions.

On their way to becoming champions, a few important life lessons were also learned, none more important or profound than the one shared by James "Big O" Brooks as he reflected on his experience on the '70-71 team.

"When you play basketball together, you realize that you really aren't that much different," Brooks said.

Epilogue

The back-to-back championship seasons in 1970 and '71 were the first two of five consecutive 20-win seasons for the Wade Hampton boys basketball team. In 1974, the Generals went 26-2 for the season and returned to the state 4A championship game, which they lost to Middleton of Charleston. In March of 1981, Coach Johnny Ross sent the following letter of resignation to his close friend and boss, school principal Lloyd Voyles, and in doing so brought an end to his 21-year tenure as head coach at Wade Hampton.

March 25, 1981

Dear Mr. Voyles:

It is with deep regret, but also with great memories that I announce my retirement as Coach of the Wade Hampton Boys Basketball Team.

I would like to thank all those who had a part in making the past 21 years a most enjoyable, exciting and rewarding time of my life.

I'm sure that every Coach dreams of winning State Championships, to coach All Americans, and win 500 games in a career, and with God's help all these things have been made possible for me.

Words cannot express my feelings for all my assistant coaches of the past and present, and all the basketball talent which came my way.

I wish to thank Mr. Voyles and all the other principals

who have been so cooperative and understanding with me
through the years and wish for them and the Basketball
Program at Wade Hampton much success in the future.
Sincerely,
Johnny Ross

Prior to a Wade Hampton basketball game on the evening of Friday, January 26, 1996, a group of former players, fellow coaches, friends and family members gathered with Coach Ross in the Wade Hampton gym to officially name the facility in Ross's honor. The physical plant of the school was demolished and rebuilt over the course of two years from 2004 to 2006, and the new gymnasium continues to be known as John W. Ross Gymnasium. A bronze plaque is mounted on the wall near the entrance of the gym, commemorating the building's dedication to Ross. A large red and white banner hangs at one end of the court recognizing the retired jersey numbers of two of Ross's star players from the 1970 and '71 teams—Clyde Mayes (55) and Jack Taylor (44).

The friendship between Norman MacDonald and Clyde Mayes that began in the Wade Hampton gymnasium in February of 1970 has now spanned nearly five decades. They played basketball, football and track together in high school and both graduated from Furman University in 1975. Mayes' 14-year professional career separated them for a time, but now both reside in Greenville. When they are together, the depth of their 50-year relationship is apparent. Their friendship serves as a tangible reminder of the good that came from the desegregation of the public schools in Greenville County.

Norman MacDonald and Clyde Mayes place their hands on the game ball from the 1970 state championship game in a recent meeting at the Clock Drive-In on Wade Hampton Boulevard in Greenville.

Wade Hampton won only one conference title between 1978 and 2000 but returned to prominence under the direction of Coach Darryl Nance who took over the program in 1997. Nance spent 19 years as the Generals' head basketball coach, and his teams won five region titles. His 2011 team recorded the school's first undefeated season (29-0) and captured the state 3A championship.

In 2015, Nance became the athletic director for the Greenville County School District and hired former Hillcrest High Coach Reggie Choplin to succeed him as the head coach and athletic director. Choplin had a successful 11-year stint as coach of Hillcrest and is the son of a former Travelers Rest High basketball coach and principal Harvey Choplin. In his first four years at Wade Hampton, Choplin's teams won a region championship (2017) and advanced to the 5A upper state final (2018), before losing to eventual state champion Dorman. Wade Hampton's girls basketball team has also enjoyed significant success in recent years, making it to the state 5A championship game in 2017 and 2018.

Nearly five decades after the forced integration of Greenville County schools, approximately 42 percent of the 2019 student population at Wade Hampton was ethnically diverse. In 2016, Wade Hampton was one of 279 schools to be named by the U.S. secretary of education as a Blue Ribbon School. SAT test scores, graduation rates and college enrollment for Wade Hampton students consistently exceed state averages and rank among the top schools in the area.

Wade Hampton graduates maintain a strong sense of pride in their school; many gather annually at class reunions to celebrate and remember their days as Generals. At least for an evening, reunion attendees are transported back to a time when life was simpler and more carefree. They remember Friday night football games, sock hops, chili cheeseburgers at the Clock Drive-In, senior cut day, prom night, their favorite teachers and a host of other memories that were created by the intersection of their lives with others on the Wade Hampton campus...and perhaps, as one of these reunions comes to a late-night close, a former cheerleader or pep club member may lead the gathered alums in the familiar rhythmical chorus of the old school fight song.

We are the Generals
Generals are we.
We're number one and all of us agree
We've got the spirit that outshines the rest

In every way in work and play Wade Hampton is the best,
And
We're Proud of our honor
Proud of our fame
Proud of our glory and loyal to our name
The red and grey will always say we stand for truth and right
Mighty Generals fight fight fight!

Author's Reflections

Walt Disney Pictures released "Remember the Titans" in the fall of 2000. The movie starred Denzel Washington as Coach Herman Boone and was based on the story of T.C. Williams High School's 1971 Virginia state football championship. The movie depicts Coach Boone taking over a racially mixed team, a by-product of the merging of three schools in Alexandria, Virginia. Boone was faced with the challenge of molding a unified team capable of winning a championship. Undoubtedly, Hollywood took some liberties, embellishing the story to enhance its entertainment value, but the movie remains one of my all-time favorites and was, in part, an inspiration for this book.

I remember walking out of the theater and thinking, "What an incredible story," but also reflecting on the fact that a similar if not slightly better story happened right here in my hometown at the very high school I attended. I thought if I ever had the time, I would attempt to write a book about Greenville's "Titans."

Like many book ideas, it was well intended but poorly executed. Then, in 2017, a student at Wade Hampton launched an online petition to permanently remove the name of General Wade Hampton from the school. She encouraged the Greenville County School Board to "leave the school's racist and unpatriotic name behind us." The petition garnered over 2,000 signatures. Concurrently, another student launched a counter-petition to keep the school's existing name and obtained a comparable number of signatures. *The Greenville News* received a plethora of letters arguing both sides of the issue, and the matter became a tool for divisiveness in our community.

Public debates were filled with passionate and compelling arguments for and against the possible renaming. Ultimately, the state legislature elected not to pursue any effort to rename the school.

In the midst of all the controversy, I could not help but think we could be encouraged by the story of Wade Hampton's 1970 and '71 championship basketball teams. Their example of putting aside differences and forming a bond while pursuing a common goal is worthy of examination in a world that seems to get a little more divided every day. History is not always positive and uplifting. History can often be hurtful and painful to reflect upon, but history can also be inspirational. The story of the *Mighty Generals* is ultimately one of inspiration.

I set out to write a book about a basketball team only to discover that I could not separate the history of our community from the story of these two teams. Research related to the content of the first two chapters of the book consumed me early on, and I was humbled by my own limited knowledge and appreciation for stories like that of the 1947 lynching of Willie Earle and the treatment of Jackie Robinson at our airport in 1959. I had teammates and friends who grew up in Nicholtown. I had driven by their neighborhood hundreds of times, yet rarely had I driven through it.

Writing the book was a personal trip down memory lane. I can still smell the popcorn at Memorial Auditorium, where I saw dozens of basketball games, attended the circus and concerts and walked across a stage to receive my high school diploma. I can hear the Wade Hampton pep band playing our fight song in a jam-packed gymnasium, and I can still feel the bone-chilling winter wind whipping through the open-air hallways of the original Wade Hampton school buildings. I was a 10-year-old running around the bleachers at Spartanburg's Red Dobson Gymnasium during the 1970 state championship tournament, and I was an 11-year-old camper sitting courtside in The Citadel's McAlister Fieldhouse in 1970 watching an epic battle between Clyde Mayes and Clyde Agnew.

I have an older brother and a younger brother, and from 1972 to 1980, at least one of us was playing basketball for Wade Hampton. My older brother Tony was the best player of the trio as he was a three-year starter on the varsity, and, along with Jack Taylor, he was co-captain of the 1974 state runner-up squad. I served as co-captain of the 1977 team, and other than the annual County Christmas Tournament, we did not win any championships that year. I was an average player at best, but my memories of playing basketball as a General become more valued with the passing of years. As I reflect on the four teams I played on at Wade Hampton, my fondness relates primarily to the relationships I formed. We were white and black and from different life paths, but we became teammates and friends. James Brooks' quote at the end of this book sums it up best: "When you play basketball together, you realize, you really aren't that much different."

As the years went by, I was fortunate to stay in contact with Coach Ross. While playing on his teams, I didn't always fully appreciate his leadership style or his coaching decisions, a view that was certainly jaded by my selfish desire for more playing time. As the years went by, however, my respect and admiration for him grew. When he passed away in 2008, his son Kelly asked me if I would deliver a eulogy at his funeral on behalf of his former players. It was an undeserved but deeply treasured honor.

I recall standing in the pulpit of Coach's home church and looking across pews filled with so many of his former players, fellow coaches, family and loved ones. Clyde Mayes and Norman MacDonald were sitting in the front row serving as honorary pallbearers. Their relationship with Coach Ross had remained strong over the years, and they both had visited him in the nursing home during his final months. Here are a few of the words I shared in paying tribute to our former coach and the leader of *The Mighty Generals*:

> *Thirty years ago, I was a member of Coach Ross's Wade Hampton High School basketball team. Back then, like some of you who played for Coach, I may not have agreed with every decision he made. I probably thought I should have played a little more or that we should have run a different offense or defense than the one he chose. But as I got older, Johnny Ross got smarter. My appreciation for his life, his accomplishments and most importantly his character grew with each passing year.*
>
> *There are three images that coincide with three character traits of Coach Ross that I will never forget.*
>
> *Humility—The first image is seeing him before practice. If you got to the gym early, you most likely would see Coach pushing a broom, sweeping the dust off the gym floor. It was a picture of his humility. Here was a man who won state championships, and yet he had no airs or ego about him.*
>
> *Self Control—There were times when I saw Coach get angry, but I never saw him lose control. I remember a time when he got really angry with me, and what I remember most about that incident was the way he expressed his disappointment to me. He called me aside,*

252

out of earshot of my teammates. I remember talking to a friend who played at another area high school, and he told me about how his coach got mad at them and the vile language he used in the locker room. I was thankful I never once heard Coach Ross use that kind of language.

Faith—His faith was what drove him to lead the kind of life he led, a life that was honoring to his Maker. He was married to the same woman all his life, committed to his family—and the last thing we always did before we hit the court was recite the Lord's Prayer.

We live in an era when so many coaches in athletics seem to be more concerned about being characters than having character. Coach Ross was a man of great character. One of Coach Ross's heroes was John Wooden, the legendary coach from UCLA. Coach Wooden used to carry a short poem around in his pocket that went like this:

> *A careful man I want to be*
> *For a little fellow follows me*
> *I dare not go astray for fear*
> *He might go the self same way.*

If you follow the example of Johnny Ross, you don't have to worry about going astray because he lived a life worthy of following. We can continue to honor him today by following the example he set for us.

A person doesn't write and self-publish a book like this one because he has any illusions of selling hundreds of thousands of copies or making any money. A small intended audience and the literary limitations of the author guarantee that a copy of this book will end up sooner than later on the 10-cent table at the thrift store. Motivation must come from a different place.

When I didn't feel like staring at microfilm or trying to string together coherent sentences, I was driven by a simple vision. I could see a student in the library at Wade Hampton picking up a copy of this book and out of curiosity taking the time to read *The Mighty Generals*. Somehow, the story would inspire them to walk across the school cafeteria one day to engage in conversation with someone who didn't look exactly like them. Maybe that person would begin to build a relationship with a person who came from a different background or establish a friendship that might move others toward a place of mutual respect for their fellow students, regardless of race or background.

A turning point for the T.C. Williams football team in "Remember the Titans" occurred when Coach Boone joined his team on an early morning run during preseason training camp at Gettysburg College in Gettysburg, Pennsylvania. While the actual movie scene was filmed at Berry College in Rome, Georgia, it was intended to depict the players running through the woods surrounding the historic Gettysburg battlefield.

After a lengthy run, a winded Coach Boone stops by a creek with a cemetery and a battlefield monument in the background. As the sun is just beginning to rise, he peers across the faces of his racially mixed team, who have been struggling throughout preseason camp to get along. He delivers the following message:

This is Gettysburg where they fought the Battle of Get-

tysburg. Fifty thousand men died in this field fighting the same fight that we are still fighting amongst ourselves. This green field right here painted red… bubbling with blood of young boys, smoke and hot lead pouring right through their bodies. Listen to their souls, men…you take a listen from the dead. If we don't come together right now on this hallowed ground, we too will be destroyed just like they were. I don't care if you like each other right now, but you will respect each other, and maybe…I don't know maybe…you'll learn to play this game like men.

I am thankful that the members of the 1970 and '71 Wade Hampton boys basketball teams were able to come together to play a game they enjoyed, develop respect for one another, build lasting friendships and in the process win championships. Let us all be inspired by the example of *The Mighty Generals.*

Appendix

1969-70 Wade Hampton Generals
Game-by-Game Results

Date	Opponent	W/L	Score	Record
12/5/69	Greer	W	60-50	1-0
12/9/69	@T.L. Hanna	L	75-58	1-1
12/12/69	Dorman	W	73-64	2-1
12/18/69 (1)	Greenville	L	67-54	2-2
12/19/69 (1)	Carolina	W	76-40	3-2
12/20/69 (1)	Easley	W	41-39	4-2
1-8-70	@Greer	L	59-56	4-3
1-9-70	@Dorman	W	64-61	5-3
1-10-70	Parker	L	61-55	5-4
1-14-70	J.L. Mann	L	66-65	5-5
1-16-70	@Spartanburg	W	58-57	6-5
1-20-70	@Greenwood	W	54-44	7-5
1-27-70	Greenwood	W	79-50	8-5
1-29-70 (1)	@Greenville	W	56-53	9-5
2-3-70	Spartanburg	W	64-60	10-5
2-6-70	@J.L. Mann	L	69-63	10-6
2-10-70	@Gaffney	W	81-55	11-6
2-13-70	@Parker	L	39-38	11-7
2-17-70	T.L. Hanna	W	68-48	12-7
2-20-70	Gaffney	W	75-67	13-7
2-21-70	Greenville	W	61-59	14-7
2-25-70 (2)	Gaffney	W	79-58	15-7
2-27-70 (2)	T.L. Hanna	W	64-55	16-7
2-28-70 (2)	Parker	W	74-60	17-7
3-5-70 (3)	A.C. Flora	W	78-48	18-7
3-6-70 (3)	Lancaster	W	76-46	19-7
3-7-70 (3)	Edmunds (Sumter)	W	60-46	20-7

Notes:

(1)   @ Greenville Memorial Auditorium
(2)   Region II 4A Tournament (at Greenville Memorial Auditorium)
(3)   4A State Championship (at Spartanburg High School)

1970-71 Wade Hampton Generals
Game-by-Game Results

Date	Opponent	W/L	Score	Record
12-3-70	T.L. Hanna	W	48-33	1-0
12-9-70 (1)	Greenwood	W	72-43	2-0
12-10-70 (1)	Parker	W	68-46	3-0
12-17-70 (1)	J.L. Mann	W	52-41	4-0
12-18-70 (1)	Carolina	W	61-45	5-0
12-19-70 (1)	Greenville	W	68-62	6-0
1-5-71	@Easley	W	54-39	7-0
1-6-71 (1)	Carolina	W	66-52	8-0
1-12-71 (1)	J.L. Mann	W	79-64	9-0
1-15-71 (1)	Greenville	W	87-60	10-0
1-16-71 (1)	Greer	W	60-40	11-0
1-19-71	@ T.L. Hanna	W	59-49	12-0
1-23-71	@Greenwood	L	69-66	12-1
1-26-71 (1)	Hillcrest	W	64-56	13-1
1-29-71 (1)	Greer	W	81-52	14-1
1-30-71 (1)	Hillcrest	W	75-52	15-1
2-2-71	@Parker	W	59-42	16-1
2-5-71	@Easley	W	83-36	17-1
2-6-71 (1)	Greenville	W	64-55	18-1
2-9-71 (1)	Carolina	W	51-40	19-1
2/12/71	@J.L. Mann	W	83-54	20-1
2/18/71 (2)	Easley	W	79-47	21-1
2/19/71 (2)	Carolina	W	73-50	22-1
2/20/71 (2)	Greenville	L	45-43	22-2
2/26/71 (3)	Spartanburg	W	80-67	23-2
2/27/71 (3)	Greenville	W	61-46	24-2
3/6/71 (4)	Dreher	W	61-53	25-2

Notes:

(1) @ Greenville Memorial Auditorium
(2) Region II 4A Tournament (at T.L. Hanna High School)
(3) 4A Upper State Tournament (at Spartanburg High School)
(4) 4A State Championship (at Carolina Coliseum, Columbia, SC)

1969-70 Wade Hampton Boys Basketball Team

Willie Allen

Horace Anderson

Johnny Ayers

Bobby Estes

Barry Foy

Tom Goodman

Clyde Mayes

Norman MacDonald

Will McNamara

Paul Myers

Levi Mitchell †

Billy Spink

James Starks

Mel Tate

Donald Wing †

Head Coach: Johnny Ross †

Assistant Coach: John Carlisle

Managers: David Watson, Danny Paterek

†- deceased

1970-71 Wade Hampton Boys Basketball Team

Doug Abrams
Buddy Asbury
James Brooks
Charlie Carter †
Larry Dodgens
Bobby Estes
Frank Fitzgerald
Clyde Mayes
Norman MacDonald
Will McNamara
Paul Myers
Steve Phillips
Billy Spink
Jack Taylor

Head Coach: Johnny Ross †
Assistant Coach: Lynn Howard

Manager: Jack Dannheisser
Trainer: Danny Paterek

†- deceased

Acknowledgments

I owe a deep debt of gratitude to many who selflessly gave of their time and talents to help this book become a reality.

To the over 40 former players, coaches, students, reporters and others who granted me an interview as part of my research: Thank you for allowing me to probe your memory from 50 years ago and for sharing your stories. For those I didn't get to talk to, I hope the book will serve to facilitate many memory-filled discussions of *The Mighty Generals*.

To the family of Coach Johnny Ross: Your willingness to support the book gave me daily encouragement to put pen to paper. For Kelly, Coach's son, thank you especially for sharing the details of your dad's life with me. You are a man of deep character and strong faith. Clearly, the apple didn't fall far from the tree.

To Ron Morris: Thank you for your patience and kindness in reading, correcting and guiding the initial drafts. I am forever indebted to you for lending your expertise in such an unselfish manner and for your continued friendship.

To Clyde Mayes and Norman MacDonald: From the very beginning, your friendship of 50 years and your connection as teammates inspired me. I enjoyed our lunches together, and thanks for sharing your memories with me.

To Ray Lattimore: I am deeply grateful for the afternoon we spent in Nicholtown retracing the footprints of your youth. Seeing the humble beginnings from which you came and knowing your incredible story moved me deeply. You are forever my teammate and friend.

To David Taylor: Thanks to another old teammate and friend for helping me make connections with people who helped shape the story and for your ongoing encouragement. Your move to Nicholtown and the impact you are having on the youth in the community sets an example for us all as we strive to build meaningful relationships across cultural barriers.

To Doug Williams: Thanks for carefully reading and editing the early drafts and for your encouragement throughout. Added thanks for being a basketball-loving friend who shares with me a deep appreciation for the artistry of a well-executed "back door cut." I think our dads would be proud that we continue to love a game that they both loved deeply.

To my parents, Frank and Lucille Chibbaro: Thank you for raising me in a home where you taught me that a person's value and worth have nothing to do with the color of their skin.

To Coach Johnny Ross, Coach Lynn Howard, Coach John Carlisle and Coach James Andrews: Thanks for not cutting me when I went out for basketball at Wade Hampton. Because you gave me a chance to be a part of a storied program, I got to wear some of the same uniforms, dress in the same locker rooms and play on the same courts as Mayes, MacDonald, Spink, Taylor and others.

To my three sons, Matt, Phillip and Nick: Thank you for putting up with a dad who likes to tell and sometimes "retell" stories. I hope your children will not grow weary of my storytelling.

To my wife, Cindy: Without your support, understanding and patience, this book would not have become a reality, and the life I get to enjoy would not be possible. I know how much you hate "clutter," so a special thanks for putting up with the mess that accompanies a three-year research project. I promise the piles of old yearbooks, newspaper clippings and interview notes will be boxed up and put out of sight...*at least for a while.*

Sources

Books

Eisenberg, John. *That First Season, How Vince Lombardi Took the Worst Team in the NFL and Set It on the Path to Glory*. Mariner Books, 2009

Gates, Henry Louis. *Stony the Road, Reconstruction, White Supremacy, and the Rise of Jim Crow*. Penguin Press, 2019

Gladwell, Malcolm. *The Tipping Point: How Little Things Can Make a Big Difference*. Little Brown and Company, 2008

Hall, J. Floyd & Bane, Garnette. *In My Wildest Dreams, The Life Story of J. Floyd Hall, Ed.D.* Press Printing Company, 2006

Robinson-Simpson, Leola Clement. *Black America Series—Greenville County, South Carolina*. Arcadia Publishing, 2007

Smith, Michael Buffalo. *The Brown Box, Remembering Greenville Memorial Auditorium*. LuLu Publishing, 2011

Stevenson, Lamont A. *Three Mountaintops, An Educator's Adventure Through Destiny*. Duncan and Duncan, Inc. Publishers, 1997

Wilkerson, Isabel. *The Warmth of Other Sons—The Epic Story of America's Great Migration*. Vintage Books, 2010

Willimon, Will. *Who Lynched Willie Earle?* Abingdon Press, 2015

Woodson, Jacqueline. *Brown Girl Dreaming.* Puffin Books, 2014

Walker, Sam. *The Captain Class, The Hidden Force That Creates The World's Greatest Teams.* Random House, 2017

Zimmerman, Samuel L. *Negroes in Greenville, 1970, An Exploratory Approach.* Greenville County Events—S.C. Tricentennial, 1970

Articles

O'Neil, Stephen. Memory, History, and the Desegregation of Greenville, South Carolina in *Toward The Meeting of the Waters: Currents in the History of the Civil Rights Movement in South Carolina during the Twentieth Century.* Edited by Winfred B. Moore and Orville Vernon. University of South Carolina Press, 2008

Newspapers

Anderson Independent
Columbia Record
Greenville Piedmont
Greenwood Index-Journal
Spartanburg Herald-Journal
Sumter Item

The Charlotte Observer
The Greenville News
The Hampton Herald
The State

Magazines

Newsweek
The New Yorker
Life Magazine
U.S. News and World Report

Other

Oral Histories, The Upcountry History Museum—Furman University, Greenville, South Carolina

About the Author

Mike Chibbaro's dream job was to work as a sports writer. His father told him to get a real job, and he became a public accountant and business consultant, spending 31 years with a Big 4 Firm. In addition to his love of sports, Mike is passionate about faith, family and leadership. When he is not doting on his grandchildren, he works as a leadership consultant and executive coach. Previously, Mike authored *The Cadillac, The Life Story of University of South Carolina Football Legend Steve Wadiak*.

Mike is a 1977 graduate of Wade Hampton High School and a 1981 graduate of the University of South Carolina. He and his wife Cindy have three grown sons and live in Greenville, South Carolina.

Mike can be contacted at mike@thirtysevenpublishing.com